'The runaway best-seller that
upped and ran away'
Radio Water Bottle

'If you want to know how footballs
came to be round not square this book
contains all you need to know'
Anon

'Ground breaking'
Groundsman's Weekly

'A perfect cure for football fever'
Society of the Wet Sponge

About the author

Bryan Gibson grew up watching football but wishing he was on the pitch rather than in the crowd. Given the chance he was asked 'What would you do if you weren't to play football?' He became a lawyer and writer including for the national press, TV and *The Stage*. This book is inspired by the many fascinating characters he met along the way.

The illustrator

Manchester-based artist, illustrator and stand-up comedian John Cooper created the images for this book. His other work includes those for *Good Moaning France: Officer Crabtree's Fronch Phrose Berk* by Arthur Bostrom. Examples of his diverse portfolio of designs, advertisements, posters and cartoons can be viewed at johncooper.org.uk

'What would you do if you weren't to play football?'

ISBN 978-1-914603-33-4 (Paperback)
ISBN 978-1-914603-34-1 (EPUB ebook)
ISBN 978-1-914603-35-8 (PDF ebook)

Published 2023 by Waterside Press Ltd
www.WatersidePress.co.uk

A catalogue record for this book can be
obtained from the British Library.

Ebook *Football's Tallest Tales* is available as an
ebook including through library models.

Football's Tallest Tales

Bryan Gibson

❈ WATERSIDE PRESS

Contents

Publisher's note

The characters, events and descriptions in the fictional parts of this book do not exist except in the author's imagination. Where real people or places are mentioned details may have been changed in the interests of the narrative. No part of the book is intended to detract from the fact that football is played by diverse individuals of every age, gender, type or ability.

To football fans everywhere especially those who would rather be on the pitch than watching in the crowd.

Peep...!
Kick Off

Magic! Abracadabra! Zim za la bim! You couldn't make it up. In the first draft of this book I included a spoof about an England team made up entirely of women who made it to a World Cup Final. I had to bin it when the Lionesses actually did. Real life catches you out. In the stories that follow I've tried to stay one step ahead. For instance did you know about Stanley Accrington who made a career out of distracting opponents, or Betty Skyrocket one of the first women footballers, or Hyam Keenbritches who was so keen about football he became Superfan of the Year three years running? I'll also let you in on the secret of how the indispensable footballer's aid Dragon Grease came about.

Before we come to these stories I need to tell you about my lamentable attempts to become a professional footballer. To be the Pelé of Pogmoor, the Dembélé of the Dearne Valley in my adopted home town of Barnsley. There's an old TV sketch in which E L Wisty compares life as a miner with that of a High Court judge. It ends 'What's more, being a miner, as soon as you're too old and tired and ill and sick and stupid...you 'ave to go. But the very opposite applies to judges—so all in all, I'd rather have been a judge than a miner'.[1] I must be one of the few people who had that choice. I escaped going down the pit by the skin of my teeth and decided not to try to become a judge because I wanted to play football. But as you'll see I did become a legal eagle even though I'd rather have joined The Eagles at Crystal Palace Football Club.

---

1. Peter Cook: https://www.youtube.com/watch?v=ofUZNynYXzM

Back to basics. If I showed you a map of the world, could you stick a pin in it where Branston is? It's at the very heart of England. Some say dead centre. There are just two things you need to know about the place. It's the home of a famous pickle. More to the point, the landlord of the Branston Arms kept goal when non-league Burton Albion were beaten 7-0 by Charlton Athletic in the Third Round of the FA Cup.[2] He used to practice using beer crates for goalposts in the days when footballers had to improvise. Facts like these do not leap from the pages of your standard almanac. But this is no ordinary football book.[3]

Branston is where I was born. A hop, skip and a hiccup from St George's Park that is now the base for all England teams. It was farmland then. There weren't world-class football pitches as far as the eyes can see. Just fields and forest. Needlewood Forest. Like Nottingham Forest or Forest Green Rovers but without the kudos. How about Needlewood Forest Nomads? That'd be quite a project for a high-rolling investor. After scaling the entire football pyramid they would eventually play in the Premier League of course. Zero emissions, pine nuts under the players' pillows, sweet dreams of truffle hunting. Trophy hunting if you prefer. Like the Ritz Hotel, football immortality is open to all. As long as a team is any good and can afford it.

I hit the ground running, breathing the same air that Harry Kane, Benfica, Galatasaray and Sligo Rovers would in years to come. You might say I was born to play football, blessed by the droplets from the local River Trent that watered the meadows reserved for football long before sprinkler systems were invented. When I was strong enough we moved to Leeds, home to sporadically successful Leeds United and fearsome players like Billy Bremner and Norman 'Bites Your Legs' Hunter. I say 'strong enough' because I could well have been blown off course as I was on the thin side. I grew tall but until I was very much older I refused to spread sideways.

2.   7 January 1956.
3.   It's also one of the few less serious books with footnotes.

Uncle Jeremiah

Leeds is where Uncle Jeremiah used to ask us riddles.

'Tell me children,' he'd say, 'one lad your age lives next door. He's got a football, a spare set of kit, some goalposts, an electric train set and a copy of the *Beano* ... The other lives 17 miles away, has nothing except a banjo with no strings, but he's a genius at football ... Who do you make friends with?'[4]

Jeremiah made footballs in his shed that he sold from a cart outside Leeds United's Elland Road ground using a sign reading

'BUY ONE, PAY FOR TWO'.

He sold one to the club but it turned out to be made of old shoe leather polished to look smart. It only lasted two minutes. It's on display in the boardroom cabinet at Leeds labelled 'Game 3,869 Matchball No 1'.

We had to do a moonlight flit after he was accused of taking the club secretary hostage and refusing to release him unless he swapped six balls for a 50 per cent stake in the tea bar.

I was still a toddler when we toddled off to Barnsley, epicentre of the Football Universe. I was fed powdered ostrich eggs. On the tin it said 'The bigger the egg the more intelligent the child's feet will become'. My parents had heard that Barnsley players bulked up on raw eggs and sherry[5] before big games so they switched to hen's eggs, being careful to serve me before pouring in the alcohol. I grew tall like a sunflower on steroids but until I was much older I remained just inches wide.

Every place has its special letter. Barnsley is registered for P. You'll see this in the coming pages. Poetry, playwrights, performers, Pogmoor, Penistone, pork pies, promotion. The words 'pillock', 'plonker' and 'prat' are all terms of endearment there.

---

4. I say make friends with the football genius. Missing banjo strings can be replaced but it's hard trying to make a silk purse out of a spoilt kid's ear.
5. Please don't try this at home or anywhere in fact.

Welcome to what I like to call the Potted North.[6] Nowadays, South Yorkshire is blessed with clean air and greenery. It's the Needlewood Forest of the Potted North an area stretching from Sheffield to Harrogate and Goole to the furthest reaches of the Snake Pass near the hamlet of Manchester. Oakwell, where Barnsley FC play, is the Wembley of the Potted North. What could be more picturesque than an oak tree and a well?

In Hampshire where I live now, there's a place called the New Forest with trees, nuts and a New Forest Football Academy for those with intelligent feet. There are acorns and water but they mostly prefer things to begin with an H or a W or preferably both. Such as Hampshire hog, Havant and Waterlooville (who played Tottenham Hotspur in the Fourth Round of the FA Cup a few years back losing 1-5) and villages like Hartley Wintney where their football ground holds 2,000 if everybody breathes in. It's what local football is all about.

One of Barnsley's favourite sons, the late Michael Parkinson[7], had a trial with Hampshire Cricket Club, so I'm not alone in coming here. It's said that he left the Potted North on a cold day with his hot water bottle and arrived in a heat wave. So he picked up his pads and headed home.[8] I got off a train to get a sandwich and stayed.

---

6. A potted down version of the North of England where they like potted meat.
7. Several people I mention went to 'my' senior school including Sir Michael. Barnsley Grammar School to be precise. When his dad died, Parky's son Mike told Radio 4 that despite his dad's anti-establishment views and humble roots he'd accepted a knighthood as it would've made 'his father in heaven smile and beam with pride' and not prevent his mum visiting the palace. I mention the connection only because of what I say about a shared sense of humour and outlook amongst local folk that must have 'rubbed off'. Gongs are not used in the text but do appear in the Index.
8. Please note the many Hs and Ws.

Things You May Not Know

Just along the road from where I'm writing this there's a sign that says 'You are now entering Jane Austen Country'. In her novel *Elm Park*,[9] written in 90 minutes plus stoppage time, Jane tells of her days coming on as a sub for Whitchurch Town. They played in crinolines[10] with two chaperones per player as she explained in her better known book *Mansfield Town*. She had a few things wrong: Mr Darcy didn't get a yellow card for taking off his shirt. Neither did he play for Corinthian-Casuals the laid back team invented two centuries later. It's not true some of her boyfriends were poor because they refused to play part-time for Andover Town and I disagree with her remark that 'Society is about balls not footballs'. Jane is buried in Winchester Cathedral. Luigi Scrosoppi, who like me wanted to be an elite footballer, is buried in another sacred place, The Vatican. He was rejected by Juventus and left Udinese after a pay dispute then had to settle for being The Patron Saint of Football instead.

Apart from the clubs I've mentioned, here in Austen territory we've got Reading, Southampton, Portsmouth, Aldershot Town, Eastleigh, Woking and Basingstoke Town. If that's not enough to worry about during *Final Score* we're close enough to watch Chelsea, Tottenham Hotspur, Arsenal, Fulham, Brentford and even West Ham United. Fortunately there's the internet where they bring it to you so that it can save gadding about. You may have heard the expression 'It's coming home' or was that to do with the World Cup?

---

9.   Then truly a park with elms in it, later Reading FC's old home ground.
10. A stiff petticoat designed to hold out a skirt (and hide the ball).

10 minutes

We arrived in Barnsley on a Yorkshire Traction bus, swapping St George's Park for Locke Park. There are no world-class pitches at Locke Park, no football pitches at all last time I looked. It's named after railway pioneer Joseph Locke who, having heard things had to rhyme, spent some of his brass on grass. The park was donated to the town by his widow Phoebe the Philanthropist who it seems wasn't all that interested in football. Did the good citizens of Barnsley not realise they were sitting on a gold mine? Sixty acres of prime football *terra firma*. Enough to see St George and Needlewood Forest off the planet. His dragon as well.

Oakwell is where the good air that wafts across Yorkshire stimulates the brain faster than laughing gas. What could be more poetic than 'It's just like watching Brazil'? This cry knocks West Ham United's 'We're forever blowing bubbles' or Liverpool's 'You'll never walk alone' into a bobble hat. I believe it escaped into the atmosphere during Barnsley's winning run towards their one and only season in the Premier League when they wore a yellow and green second strip matching Brazil's colours. Plus of course their similar styles of play. I've got the t-shirt. I wear it in bed.

It's not just Brazil who wear yellow. I can't think of this dazzling colour without being reminded of Norwich City who have Captain Canary for a mascot and eat mustard on toast before every game. Celebrity chef Delia Smith is a main shareholder there.

Elton John and the Grimsby Police XI

Many clubs have famous backers. This started long before Ryan Reynolds and Rob McElhenney popped up in Wrexham from Hollywood and made a struggling club ultra famous using a syndicated digital stream showing their quest for the Sunny Uplands. Beat that for a tale!

One of the earliest was Elton John, former chair at Watford FC. It's not generally known that he wrote 'Candle in the Wind' one blustery evening when the floodlights failed. His 'Bennie and the Jets' refers to Barking and Dagenham FC[11] and one of his early songs 'Grimsby' is a tribute to that town's Police XI who I mention elsewhere in this book.

In my two decades in the Potted North there was a good deal of muck and the stone buildings hadn't yet been steam cleaned. There are no pits there now apart from heritage sites and sealed up mine shafts.[12] It used to be a place where miners held contests to see who could burn their monthly free ton of coal fastest. Even throughout the summer. 'Just like baking in Benidorm'. More annoyingly there were some good players at Barnsley FC to keep me out of the team, not just those Michael Parkinson mentioned in his book *Football Daft*, when he claimed that if they needed a new player they'd 'whistle down the pit and take the first man up'. Coal rhymes with goal as well (and so does Devante Cole their modern day scoring wizard). The club has always nurtured talented youngsters. It's a complete mystery why they ignored me.

Locals the world over are full of witticisms but in Barnsley it's an acute condition, an art form. 'Just like watching Brazil' is the tip of an iceberg. Award winning poet and broadcaster, Ian McMillan has

---

11. Like many community clubs The Jets field a range of teams including Little Flyers for ages 4 to 6 and Wildcats sessions for girls 5 to 11.
12. But there *are* glassworks—the town's other traditional industry—now celebrated in the Glass Works retail hub.

filled a small library writing books about it. He even produced a volume called *It's Just Like Watching Brazil*. I know McMillan doesn't begin with a P. The letter M's near enough for me and there's an N at the end of his first name which is closer still. One of the first things you learn as a lawyer is that *everything is approximate*. Like time, distance, colour and weight. That if a witness says, 'I saw a man with a blue cap driving a red car at 9 o'clock' it's your job to convince them it was a purple lorry, a woman in a green sun hat, and close to midnight. When we qualify we're given a starter kit of 'maybes', 'possibles' and a box of 'depends'.

Ian McMillan has become a torchbearer for the Potted North and well beyond. The host of Radio 3's *The Verb* and often seen or heard on other programmes, he's styled Poet in Residence at Barnsley FC. He also holds such a role at English National Opera and has written opera in dialect. Par for the course in Barnsley you might say but still leading the other poets, playwrights and performers by a head or two. He'll probably be asked to be Poet Laureate and given a butt of sherry. Maybe he can revive the practice I've mentioned by giving it to Barnsley FC with a box of eggs. I've steered away from dialect in this book except when quoting people or where I'm on safe ground. Except in short bursts I've not tried to make the text rhyme but my story about Pundit Wars is based on the language of football commentators and how they enjoy literary immunity.

Room at the Top (of Any League)

One scribe who lived near Barnsley was the author John Braine. He was the librarian at a place called Darton. He said he and his wife couldn't possibly bear to live in the town itself. A typical local riposte might have been,

'Tha's not from rand [around] here, so what's it got to do wi thee?!'

But this leading kitchen sink writer did say what lovely folk Barnsley people were (and they are). He was careful to add that they'll also share your sandwich on a train journey. Braine always was a bit of a snob which wouldn't have taken him far in Barnsley Market.

Room at the Top, his most famous novel featuring the social misfit Joe Lampton was written in Darton in-between handing out library books. The rumour is that in the first rough of the story Lampton was a tripe-seller with his sights set on a yacht in Monte Carlo. The tragic Alice Aisgill played the lead with Wombwell Thespians and they lived in a place called Spion Kop Behind the Goal. The idea of there being room at the top also gave hope to many football clubs with an eye on promotion but the bottom line is that it is all about the downside of misplaced ambition, how reaching for the stars has a flip side. I should've read it before thinking I might have a football career not years afterwards.

As I've said the law wasn't my first choice of career. When I discussed my need to earn a crust with the lady careers officer at the Town Hall I think she was perplexed. I'll call her Ms Pinkerton because we were formal in those days.

'What job are you thinking of?' enquired Ms Pinkerton.

'I want to be a footballer … I think I'm living in the right place. Sooner or later they'll come knocking … perhaps you can speed up the inevitable … Tell them about my football heritage. My Uncle Jeremiah once supplied a matchball to Leeds United and a distant cousin supports Partick Thistle.'[13]

Who could say no to a lad from the very sod of where the England team would pitch up?[14] Ms Pinkerton did.

'No,' she said, followed by 'I'm afraid we don't have any vacancies at all under Footballer.'

I stressed to her that I lived just a quick sprint from Oakwell and that I was happy to forego my testimonial match at the end of ten years but even that didn't cut any ice. I let her rummage in her files.

---

13. Comedian Billy Connolly famously said they're called Partick Thistle Nil.
14. Pardon the pun, but pitch and pun begin with P so too good to miss.

She found me a job under W with Wilthorpe Window Cleaning Company. It lasted three days before I left saying I'd no head for heights. Just for football heights. Not best pleased, Ms Pinkerton rummaged again. She found me something under NCB for National Coal Board. I'd train to be a manager. The catch was that in the meantime I had to go down the mine. I don't know what my qualifications had to do with this. They were mostly on the arts side. I'd concentrated on English Literature so I'd be able to converse with the writers and poets in the area.

> **I'M SORRY WE CAN'T SHOW YOU THIS.** We seem to have half a dozen pitch invaders who are not wearing much more than their own smiles. There'll be a short break in play whilst the stewards recover garments and organize a jumble sale. But I've got time to tell you a Tall Tale...

Tall Tale No. 1
Stanley Accrington

Sports master and breeder of prize winning budgerigars Algernon Feathers was shocked when he heard the news that the school team had lost 1-0.

'Now young Stanley... Do I have this right... I'm told you were the one who distracted Ronnie Cloggs the goalkeeper when he let in that goal yesterday. Whose side are you on?'

Good footballers need certain attributes: intelligent feet (or at a pinch at least one well-schooled left or right foot), eyes that swivel front and back, and the ability to play without the ball so long as they have a rough idea where in the world it may be. Those destined for mega-stardom tend to have extra skills such as the ability to disappear in a cloud of dust after making a tackle and the capacity to trick opponents into making bad decisions. It helps a great deal if they are born with Football Brain which is a condition that helps to connect these and other tools of the trade together.

Football Brain afflicts eleven out of ten children. Its earliest symptoms include involuntary kicking movements in the womb and an inability to think about anything else but football once a child has been weaned onto solids. The condition peaks between ages 12 and 19, depending on who you ask. Nowadays it can be detected using litmus paper and a light dressing of salad cream. New mothers are handed a fact sheet by midwives.

Stanley Accrington was fortunate. He was born with an extra gene that allowed him to divert attention, confuse folk and propel them in the wrong direction. That's why he was packed off to the Distraction Academy in his teens on a scholarship where he became the first student to be awarded the academy's Gold Medal for Duping a Flat Back Four. Even so, this star pupil was asked to leave a term early due to the effect his disruptive antics had on other students. This left them at sixes and sevens every time he let fly with the tricks he had up his sleeve. By then though, he'd learnt several other things: That skill alone is never enough if you want to be a footballer; that you still have to be spotted; also that there are thousands upon thousands of competent footballers so that whoever you are it still helps if you know someone in the game or come across a club on a tight budget that's desperate for players. I'll come to all of this.

Towards the end of his playing career Akkers told football newspaper *Sporting Dollop* how he first learned about the need for a leg-up and that he had the extra gene in him.

'My very first football memory is from when I was at junior school…I noticed activity down in the local park. It turned out we were playing another school. One of my classmates Ronnie Cloggs was in goal. There were no nets in those days, just goalposts and a bent crossbar, so I stood right next to him on what would have been the goal line, if they'd had any whitewash, and we chatted.

"What y'doing, Clogger?"

"Playing in goal."

"What's going on, why are you on your own?"

"I'm not on my own…Wait and see."'

Akkers explained that Ronnie had pointed into the distance and said, 'See, there in the mist…that's us.' Squinting hard Akkers could make out other kids who seemed to be from the year above him and his classmate Ronnie. None of the other kids in their year had been told about the match. Akkers wondered why Ronnie was so clogging special.

'How come I'm not playing Clogger?' he'd asked.

'Not picked,' Ronnie had replied, 'I was chosen by Algie Feathers, our sports master, the one who breeds budgies in his spare time.'

That evening Akkers told his dad Fred what had transpired.

'Right,' said Fred, 'Old Feathers that's what it's all about. He's Ronnie's dad's second cousin twice removed and he's taken a shine to young Ronnie... Someone must have whispered in Feather's ear, the remaining one not the one a crazed budgie chewed off, and Feathers must have said Ronnie could start out in goal and work his way up to centre forward... He must have let him begin a year before everyone else.' It turned out that Ronnie's dad used to play for Slack Bottom Rovers Reserves, so yes he'd had a word in Feathers' good ear and he had indeed let Ronnie have a go in the school team.

Akkers explained to his dad Fred that by the time the ball reached them Ronnie had become wrapped up in their little chat. 'He'd completely forgotten why he was there... The ball whizzed past both of us as we glanced sideways at it. Our school lost 1-0 and I think I'm going to be in trouble... Ronnie's thinking of changing his name to Not So Clever Cloggs.' That was the seismic moment when Fred uttered a few short words of advice to young Akkers that seared into and livened up his dormant football brain: 'It's not who you know, it's who you grovel too... and the reason he let in a goal is called *distraction*.'

'You learn something every day,' thought Akkers, his re-engaged football brain burning brightly as he stared at a photo of a player doing a bicycle kick. He took to practicing this until he mastered the technique, hoping that before his teenage spots disappeared he would be spotted. He learnt more distracting moves, harnessing his natural talent. At first, by kicking a tin can around the street outside, then dribbling with a hollowed-out melon stuffed with dusters and finally a real football which he won in a raffle after distracting the woman picking the numbers. In between kicking the ball around he would distract pedestrians by asking them the way to the nearest lamp post or raising a finger towards the sky and saying, 'There's a lot of orange juice in the clouds tonight'. Every day he prayed he'd be seen by a talent scout. Preferably one who knew his dad or Aunt Freda. Someone to give him a leg-up. To help him jump the queue. Even better if it was someone who understood what distraction was all about.

So it happened that Bill, the husband of Rosie Bluebottle who Akkers' dad fancied a bit and had once given up his seat on a bus for, turned the corner. Just as young Akkers headed the ball through the window of Ray Haddocks Fish & Chips. 'Now, now. Magic. Smashing, that's just smashing. We're looking for a player daft enough for that,' said Bill Bluebottle. Bill just happened to be chief scout for Ramrod Rovers and Akkers' career was about to get up and running. The rest of course is history.

'Some people have a goal in them,' Bill Bluebottle advised Stan Kettledrum, owner of Ramrod Rovers. 'Others just have bits of human tissue, bones, organs, muscles and so on. But young Akkers has a goal in him. All we need to do is bottle it. It's bursting to pop into the world and hopefully when it does he'll be in the six-yard box playing for Ramrod Rovers.'

Kettledrum knew that Bill Bluebottle was good at bottling things so took him at his word. 'Has he got a throw-in in him?' enquired Kettledrum, 'Is there a corner lurking deep down inside? Does he have a tackle in him?' Then hoping for a positive answer, 'Does he do ... *distraction*?' A stout man with a big ego who only usually attended matches to collect the takings, Kettledrum almost fell off his chair with excitement when Bluebottle told him about Akkers winning a Gold Medal at the Distraction Academy. Normally, the receipts pocketed, he'd head home by the fastest route before the players got wind of the money. But the thought of Akkers signing for Ramrod Rovers for the price of a bottle top stopped Kettledrum in his tracks.

'Should we X-ray his insides or can we take them as red?'

'They're red alright and some of them a bit pink ... He knows where the goal is ... and the way to the ground,' replied Bill. 'He just needs a window of opportunity after smashing the one belonging to Ray Haddocks ... Yes, he *distracts* everybody he comes across and has done so most of his life ... Where does he sign?'

So began a stellar career in football. First with Ramrod Rovers then Minster United. After that with Minster City, Minster Monsters and abroad with Milano Minestrone who'd won 57 trophies in three seasons. There Akkers honed his skills and ate chilli and peppers until he was a seasoned player. Coaxing goals from his innards and distracting everybody he came across. In no time at all he could takes eight players in one direction whilst the ball spun in the other. He simply pointed at the sky and said, for example, 'Looks like we're in for a storm'.

He became a master of his own natural ability, taking the art to new levels of mayhem and befuddlement. 'It's easy,' he once told Radio Water Bottle. 'I just stand there as if there's no tomorrow then point out the pigeons on the frame of the floodlights and say something unexpected like "Do you happen to have any peanuts with you?" … it comes naturally to born distractionists, not so easily to those who have to make friends with magicians or pickpockets to learn how tricks work.'

To this day Stanley Accrington holds the record for the highest number of distractions per game that experts say is 139, 140 or 93 depending on how you do the maths. Akkers played in seven internationals during seven years for seven countries so distracted were those who checked his Football Brain annual renewal certificates, always donning size seven boots, wearing shirt No. 77 and carrying out a minimum of seven distractions every seven minutes.

With bonuses and after ten seasons he was flush enough to buy his first football boots and stopped playing in flip flops, which other players found distracting. By then he could mesmerise opponents at the drop of a bag of pork scratchings, a trick he used after discovering how keen they were to stop and pick them up. Another he learned from veteran footballer Barry Tone, the Wizard of Wildebeest Wanderers, of creeping up behind opponents and growling like a bear then nipping under their radar as they spun round. If not picked to play from the start, he'd frequently be subbed on in response to fans chanting 'Stan, Stan, we want Stan, bring on Stan the Distraction Man'. He'd then proceed to upset the opposition. Forever he remained committed to his forte as he explained in his multi-million selling autobiography *The Dark Art of Distraction*, the bible on the subject used by every club in the land. 'Stick to what you're good at' he would tell young players. 'I was good at distraction and careful not to get self-distracted.'

In his twilight years, Akkers played for Solar Wednesday every Tuesday or it may have been Bankrupt Thursday every Friday. He was pursued by various dead end clubs but never tempted out of retirement. As he reminded folk when he collected his Lifetime Achievement Award for Bewilderment, 'I owe Ronnie Cloggs an awful lot…I was born distracting people but had it not been for that day on the school playing field I might never have confused managers, players, my own team, opponents and the few friends I have alike. I might well have wasted my energy powering floodlights or the manager's kettle and that would have meant going off at a complete tangent from what football's all about.' But by then the gathering had been completely distracted by the real hero of the hour, Bill Bluebottle, who this time around hadn't spotted a new player to sign for Ramrod Rovers but was chasing a loudly buzzing hornet that he was trying to swat with a rolled up copy of *Sporting Dollop*.

Stanley was completely lost for words when folks turned their attention back to him. He wasn't used to something else grabbing the limelight. But he did manage to muster his thoughts and tell the audience how humble he felt to have been born with the extra gene that most kids' Football Brains don't contain.

'Smashing, smashing … We need someone as daft as you!'

Play resumes . . .

15 minutes

We . . . I'm now adopting the football supporters' 'we'. 'We' frequently lose. More precisely we just 'miss out'. We're sometimes not good in the 97th minute.

The bookmakers of this world make a tidy living offering long odds on a Barnsley victory. When they beat Port Vale 7-0 in the opening game of the 2023–24 season it was reported that bookies were scurrying off and hiding in the woods. We did have a good season a few years ago when we mastered the high press under former Wolfsburg coach Valérien Ismaël. Going from zero to Nero in six months to return to the Championship. The high press is a zonal system in which everyone including the goalkeeper goes on all-out attack in the opposing team's six yard box. It wasn't invented by Ismaël but by the kids at our junior school who went on the attack 30 at a time or 34 if those with their heads stuck in the railings worked themselves free.

Don't Forget Your TV Licence

If you want to know how to look fierce on the pitch stand by the mirror holding a picture of Ismaël. Be careful to put on an oven glove so as to make sure you don't burn your hand whilst holding the image and mimic his stare. I wanted to insert his photograph in this book but the printers ran off shouting 'Help!' so I've included a link to one the BBC use to scare viewers into coughing up for TV licences.[1]

---

1.   https://www.bbc.co.uk/sport/football/60149753

As I write this we're back down in League One and marking time for an assault on the Sunny Uplands. I've watched when we beat top sides including Manchester United, Tottenham Hotspur, Chelsea and Liverpool. Then lost to lower league Altrincham, Gateshead Town and Tranmere Rovers. No-one can fathom it.

The Potted North has many famous football teams. Sheffield United, Sheffield Wednesday, Leeds United, Doncaster Rovers, Rotherham United, Chesterfield and Harrogate Town. Lots of smaller ones too. They all have a rude heritage (some ruder than others). Most of them are Barnsley's closest rivals depending on who you listen to and what day of the week it is. Along with Huddersfield Town. Another side that doesn't always know a good footballing prospect. I'll come to that.

As I've said, I wanted my passport to say 'Footballer'. I used to play whenever I could. I suppose that like many kids I was football mad. Even though Ms Pinkerton at the Town Hall never did match me up with The Tykes I was determined to keep knocking on the door. Once I had a job at the pit there was always a chance that, Parkinson-style, they would whistle down and I'd be the first man up. I planned to stand by the foot of the shaft at the ready. Only I never went down. During my first week at Carlton Colliery a miracle occurred. I was busy learning to 'locker up' pit tubs, throwing a stick into their spokes as they sped by, when I got a message to say a letter had arrived at home. It had a football emblem on the envelope. I sped there after work and opened it in trepidation. It wasn't from Barnsley FC but another Yorkshire club.

The reprieve came with a day to go before I'd have descended the mineshaft. Instead I had trials with two leading Yorkshire clubs. Hull City, who sent me the letter I've mentioned and closer to my home Huddersfield Town. Instead of a quick sprint to Oakwell, I went traipsing off all around the Humber Estuary to what was then Hull's Boothferry Park Stadium. It took hours. There wasn't a direct route or a bridge over the River Humber at that time. There was even a ditty about that: 'Will they ever bridge the Humber, will they ever bridge it o'er, is it always the exception to the rule'. It was however re-assuring to discover there were poets in Hull.

20 minutes

As the carriages trundled past Goole Town AFC[2] before travelling all the way to the east coast on the other side of the River Humber, I caught a glimpse of their players doing slow stretches and this must have sent me to sleep. I drowsed off thinking of the last minute advice my parents had given to me as I left home for the first time.

'Don't go breaking a leg', Mum said.

Dad was even more pragmatic. 'You'd be better off playing cricket ... cricketers have longer careers ... you'll regret playing football'.

Learning to Swear Like a Footballer

Still wondering about early redundancy as a footballer and the sweet smell of cricket bats doused in linseed oil tempting me to swap my ticket for one to Yorkshire's ground at Headingley, in my dreamy state I made out the words across the front of a desk as it swirled into view: 'The Greatest English Poet of the 20th Century'.

The guy seated behind the desk looked vaguely like Eric Morecambe of Morecambe and Wise fame. He greeted me with the words, 'Hello young man, my name's Phillip. Welcome to Larkinland ... Don't you be put off by what your parents told you. I've written a poem about what parents do to their kids. Maybe I'll let you read it when you're old enough ... I hear you're on your way to Hull where I'm in charge of cursing and swearing.'[3]

'Before you play football with seasoned professionals you need to learn a thing or two about rough language. See that chart ... Right, starting with B and moving down, what does it say? Here, borrow my specs ... and tell me what F, S and W say'. We went through every line and he was just handing me a book and saying, 'Now, chuff off and read my latest collection' as we pulled into Hull Railway Station.

---

2. Now AFC Goole, The Vikings.
3. For those who *are* old enough see Larkin's poem 'This Be The Verse'.

Exhausted, my football boots sticking out of my bag so they'd recognise me, the way spies pick out each other in busy places, I said 'Hello' to the young player who'd been sent to greet me and who knowing how to read a game of football had spotted me in a flash without even turning round to look. 'Man on' is the expression, I believe.

When we reached the huge green edifice of a stadium the first thing they did was take one look at my slim frame and arrange to feed me. Where else could you arrive for work on day one in a plum job, nervous, completely hyped up and ready to go, and be mistaken for a beanpole? I was still as thin as a rake, a slighter version of Peter Crouch, not someone solid like Wayne Rooney, Paul Gascoigne or Adebayo Akinfenwa of Wycombe Wanderers. A Will O' the Wisp who could ghost past opponents but had to avoid bumping into them in case I got flattened or they breathed on me.

'Take the lad down to Luigi's and get some pasta into him,' said manager Cliff Britton pulling a neatly folded pound note out of a tin box and handing it to the guy who met me at the station. 'Get a good sleep and come back fresh in the morning.' It turned out not to be St Luigi, Patron Saint of Football, but Pier Luigi's, a well-known Italian diner, where I discovered that not all spaghetti comes out of a can.

Next morning I made my waif-like but more well fed way to the dressing-room where I met with my first taste of professional football banter. 'Don't they get owt to eat in Barnsley?' … 'Is that why they're heading for the drop? Have they sent us some dripping[4] that's spare to requirements' … 'A streak of it' … 'Stand sideways, let's have a better look?' That was my entry settled in the Roll of Footballer's Nicknames where all players must register using two syllables at most. 'Get your boots on Streaky and don't slip down them sluice grates by the pitch.' Remarkable when I look back. Nowadays people ask me whether I used to be a rugby prop forward, especially if I wear my threadbare Marks & Spencer hooped shirt that I've preferred since it was given to me 15 years ago.

---

4.   I'm not sure how familiar all readers may be with dripping but it's what drops into the pan from a roast. We ate it on toast if we couldn't get caviar.

The only thing the Hull players talked about was football. I've since discovered it's a general affliction amongst elite footballers.[5] Football, football, football, non-stop, fills their waking hours. Maybe gambling gets a look in here and there. Occasionally I heard the Hull players ask each other, 'Did you get a jump last night?' I guessed it had something to do with leaping for the ball. There were no entries under J for Jump on Phillip Larkin's wall chart. Otherwise his list came in more than useful.

The players were paranoid about their arch-rivals Grimsby Town, though they always had an eye on the fact that a one-time Chief Constable of Grimsby, Charles Butler,[6] ran a unique scheme for ex-professional footballers seeking to eke out their playing careers. He recruited them as police officers. Stacked with ex-pros, Grimsby Borough Police XI won every competition going. Butler was the Alex Ferguson of policing and his legacy passed from chief constable to chief constable. The men in his force were exceedingly fit and top of the league when it came to the day job of chasing criminals. It is said burglars would stop them and ask for autographs.

I'd been spotted by a football scout, a Scottish guy called Jimmy Baxter, who'd played for Dunfermline and in an FA Cup Final for Preston North End. Alongside the great Tom Finney. Jimmy then ran a newsagents in Barnsley, for whom he also played, but went talent spotting. His pal Cliff Britton had just taken over as manager at Hull. Britton played with Bristol Rovers and Everton and won the FA Cup with the latter, before going on to manage Burnley, Everton, Preston North End and then Hull. Despite his immense track record, he was as easy going as they come and had a pleasant way with all his players: good, bad, indifferent and me.

I knew I might be in with a chance as I'd grown up alongside lads who went on to play for top clubs, win league titles and FA Cup medals, even represent England. Among them were Jimmy Greenhoff

---

5. Eric Cantona said 'Often there are players who have only football as a way of expressing themselves and never develop other interests'.

6. I discovered only recently that Charles Butler also went to the same school as I did. I was pleased he chose a career beginning with P for Policing.

('the finest player never to play for England' and scorer of the winning goal in an FA Cup Final) and his younger brother Brian, both of whom played for Manchester United (and in Jimmy's case a long time with Stoke City). Brian played 18 times for England, 17 times more than I did, but I'll come to that.[7] They were both great players, Jimmy being especially electric, charismatic and easy to pick out with his shock of naturally blonde hair. I never understood why neither of them wanted to play for their home town club, not even on the way up or back down again.

25 minutes

From the moment I arrived in Hull I found it strange. I was probably homesick (which wasn't helped by Phillip Larkin having mentioned my parents). Feeling on your own isn't good when dealing with the banter of a charged dressing-room. Nor wandering around in a strange place with time on your hands because footballers can have a short working day. In my spare time I went down to the city's docks and years before Manchester United legend and poet Eric Cantona I discovered that (in his words) 'When the seagulls follow the trawler, it's because they think sardines will be thrown into the sea'. But there's no room for excuses in football and playing with wary strangers lends you an element of surprise.

The Curious Couple Who Did Football Digs

I was looked after by an eclectic middle-aged couple, let's call them Jim and Jenny, who did football digs and made me feel welcome. They were in a feud with Littlewoods Pools over a Treble Chance ticket with which they were convinced they'd won £75,000 (over £2 million today). Their coupon had somehow 'got stuck in the post box' and went uncollected.

---

7.   Again Jimmy and Brian went to the same school as I did.

The experience seemed to have eaten into their very existences. Bottom line is they didn't have a leg to stand on against Littlewoods or the Post Office. There was no hard evidence Jim had posted the coupon.

Jim and Jenny claimed they'd placed their Xs next to the same numbers on their football coupon every week and that they'd done this for ten or more years, which unfortunately didn't mean a thing, legally speaking, nor to Littlewoods' public relations department. Together in the same billet, along with another young football hopeful, we listened dutifully to their grousing, at every meal, while watching TV and in their well tended garden.

Maybe it was something to hold on to, a tale they could tell their more affluent friends, an excuse for their modest station in life. Jim didn't seem like a con-man, but they never do. Jenny wore the trousers and maybe, just maybe, he was scared to death when the results were declared each Saturday, or the pair could have been in it together, even afflicted by what lawyers call *folie à deux*,[8] and were conspiring to defraud the pools company. Was the story true at all or completely made up for a lark and then they got stuck with it? If they really did lose out what extraordinary bad luck.

I was keen to leave Jim and Jenny to their woes, play football, then speed off home to regale my friends with stories about the players I'd met and not that my landlord and landlady had lost out on the pools. I discovered that there is more to football than being any good at it. You have to handle things. I was probably seen as an interloper come to disturb the regular players' peace and quiet. I thought I was gift wrapped but if I stood sideways I all but disappeared. The better professionals seemed to be stocky with a low centre of gravity. Here was this lamp post of a player who shone a light on nothing very much. The manager had invited me but they were adept at hospital passes and delivering balls just out of reach to make any newcomer

---

8. Madness of two people who are perfectly sane apart.

look inept. Placing themselves in awkward positions when you were looking for someone to pass the ball to.

One evening there was a special game when pros mixed with trainees. The pros all seemed to disperse like rats from a sinking ship whenever a trainee got the ball. Clever tricks really and I suppose it was their jobs on the line if Hull signed any of us. I once saw how top professionals can do just the opposite if they want to when Liverpool FC played a charity match and covertly included a complete novice. They made him look good by 'playing to him' creating spaces and ensuring he was in the right place at the right time. They even arranged for him to score at the end of a run of passes. The way a marching band adjusts to the horses, not the other way around. Who was this streak of a lad? Was he a cutting from Jack's beanstalk in the pantomime at Barnsley's Theatre Royal?[9] 'Who's that bespectacled phantom on the touchline who looks like Eric Morecambe?' I diverted myself. 'The one furiously scribbling down the player's four letter words?'

There were some friendly players such as Chris Chilton who scored over 220 goals for the club, and the supporters' favourite Ken Wagstaff. Chilton had turned down a move to Tottenham Hotspur amongst interest from other leading clubs. Only after staying with Hull for many years did he 'ease up' playing for Coventry City and then Bridlington Trinity. Ken Wagstaff was Hull's record signing at the time for £40,000, from Mansfield Town. A strong, burly player he was voted 'The Greatest to play for Hull' by their supporters. I spent several frosty mornings sending the ball in to Ken, who'd flick it onto Chris who'd volley it past a spring loaded plywood goalkeeper. Time and again. I saw the move rewarded twice in a 2-0 league win the following Saturday. That's professional football for you. 'One from the training ground' as the commentators say (and that as you'll read later scores decent points in a game of Pundit Wars).

---

9.   The top venues may now be The Lamp Room and Civic Hall. I played five-a-side for Barnsley Boys Club which met in the building where the first is now. We never contradicted those who thought we were from Barnsley FC.

After training it was down to the pub for several pints of beer and 20 Park Drive cigarettes. The tipped variety, which I think was the players' grudging nod towards healthy living. I was more used to downing a non-alcoholic concoction in Gordon Pallister's smoke free Temperance Bar in Barnsley's Back Regent Street. Pallister was an ex-Barnsley player, a full back, who put in over 200 appearances for the club then opened a place that would give Harry's Bar in Venice a run for it's money in terms of ambience even if Gordon's alcohol free fruit cocktails differed from Harry's famous vodka martinis. Before that Pallister was with Bradford City. There was a certain frisson for a young football hopeful when served by the great man.

Hull City manager Cliff Britton was thoroughly decent about things when we agreed that I'd leave after a month. Nothing to do with my light frame, he assured me, as he took a last quizzical look at me. He made it seem like it was my choice entirely. That they wanted me even though they didn't, were unlucky I wasn't happy to stay. The good thing was that I'd been with the first team squad and seen moves on the training ground that I was able to copy in matches back home. Nothing in life is ever wasted.

I found it hard to look Jimmy Baxter in the face next time I saw him. He'd gone out of his way to help. I believe he got the rocket up him that I didn't. He was a lovely guy and Barnsley were fortunate to have him for a couple of seasons at the end of his playing days, and only because his wife came from the town and wanted to be 'back home'. Before I left for Hull he'd called round unexpectedly one evening to check that it was okay with my parents. I was just 16 going on 17 at the time. Under his arm he had a photograph album and a thick folder of press cuttings which we spent the evening pouring over and listening to his life story. The glossiest and most impressive pictures were of him in action at Wembley in the FA Cup Final. That's when I made the mistake of asking him something I should have known the answer to. A couple of important things you learn as a lawyer is not to do this or to put words in your client's mouth since the wrong answer can lead to you looking like a fool and evidence that you've suggested to your own witness is worthless.

'Did you win?' I asked Jimmy.

'It's not about winning, it's about the occasion,' he replied as he took his loser's medal from a box in his pocket, the smallest hint that his eyes were glazing over.[10]

It was never the same after I let him down at Hull. Homesick or not.

> CHAOS IN THE CENTRE CIRCLE with what looks like a hamstring injury on one side, concussion on the other and the referee flat on her back after slipping on the over-watered grass. The fourth official is trying to pick up the pieces and this could be a lengthy interruption…

---

10. Preston lost 3-2 in 1954 to West Bromwich Albion.

Avoiding the curse of self-distraction can be critical in
the era of smartphone-induced micro-attention spans.

Tall Tale No. 2
Superfan

M any football fans keep to a strict routine. Hyam Keen-britches also likes to absorb every known footballing fact. He needs to check out each and every encyclopedia of football knowledge, double check it for accuracy and carry out a series of further checks. These include an auto-check, a fact-finding check and putting on his favourite checking outfit (a check jacket, check trousers, check shirt) and sitting under an umbrella with checks on it before ensuring all previous checks have been carried out. His life is perfectly ordinary at other times but on match day he keeps to the same drill. He never deviates. This has been checked out.

If Hyam's beloved Chunter United are playing at home he chunters with best of them. Chunter fans chunter long and loud about everything: the manager, the players, the pitch, the score and the half-time five-a-side games between teams of Little Checkers and Little Chunterers. His team's Worthless Insurance Policy Stadium has become a mecca of chuntering. Hyam leads the fans in their pre-match warm up when the place is a hive of checking and chuntering.

If Chunter United are playing away—however near or whatever the distance—Hyam puts his head down at 5.17 pm the evening before, no sooner no later, ready for an early start. Until recently, as we will learn, he would travel to games on his electric bike which he charged from a lamp post in the street before sending a bag of peanuts to his local council offices with the massage, 'Sorry, I can't help myself. I'll call mid-week to check that you've received this gift'. He calls the bike 'Trigger' after a horse he saw during a Festival of Old Movies at the Chunter Fleapit Multiplex (he'd gone there to check out the place naturally). But there is no entertainment on the evening before a match home or away. 'Oh, no, I must keep myself in check' he tells those who are prepared to listen.

Equipped with an excessive knowledge of results, players and games played by Chunter United, Chunter Reserves, Chunter B, Chunter Lilies (the town's ladies team) and most clubs in the universe dating back decades before the dawn of time, Hyam is the fountain of all checked out football knowledge. As keen as they come, he has followed Chunter United when playing friendly games against the lowest of opposition and on tours to the foothills of far continents, remote parts of the jungle and the Check Republic. During spells when planes have been grounded during natural disasters he has still arrived early. When the only route was by sailboat during a hurricane, a trip on a mountain bus (of which there may have been one a month) followed one after another by rides on a team of donkeys he has always found time to check out the local sights before the game. He loves it when the other side play like the donkeys he arrived on though his recurring nightmare is having to tell people, 'I wasn't there'.

Chunter United are not a 'big club'. They have a modest playing squad who wear numbers 1-29, allowing for unused ones such as unlucky No. 13, and No. 9. The first of these the club can't give away. The second is reserved for the president's son who is expected to sign for the club on a ten year contract as Chunter's highest paid player a day before his dad is elbowed out. Keenbritches keeps a tight check on how much the players earn, how much they spend at supermarket check outs, their outlay at Chunter Racecourse and anything else that is capable of being checked. Winner of last year's reality show *Excess Knowledge in a Foreign Football Field*, Keenbritches was interviewed for an edition of *Chunter Hunter* the club fanzine and described his routine.

'I wear the club colours, red, white and blue except for my socks which are green to match those of the goalkeeper. My tie and bracers are also multicoloured but my handkerchief has purple and green stripes to symbolise the colours worn by the club in its early years. I'm not superstitious but I put everything on in a set order. This is determined by when in the game Chunter United last scored a goal from which I deduct stoppage time. I put my hat on first followed by one shoe, then I balance on my left leg whilst putting on the rest of my clothes checking that every single stitch matches our club's colours. At this point I hop around the room, put on my remaining shoe and check three times that I've switched off the light. If I happen to see an animal coming towards me as I head for the game, such as a mouse scurrying along the pavement, a stray warthog, or a police horse, I go back and start all over again. I have a season ticket for home games, so I always sit in the same seat. At away games I try to sit in Row E and if available seat 26. If that is taken, I attempt to persuade the occupant to move, but I only apply mild force unless greater leverage and a pepper spray works.'

Hyam explained that his routine continues throughout the game. 'I carry two slices of pork pie which I eat at half-time unless my team is winning 3-0 in which case I keep the second slice until full-time. The small sachet of tomato sauce I keep in my pocket untouched. I toss this into a waste bin on the way out for luck. I get dizzy if I don't do it. My flask of coffee I may drink at any time but not at all if it goes cold when I pour it discreetly down a drain after checking that no-one is looking. My socks I pull up every 30 seconds, something I've noticed others do, so that it ripples along the row like a Mexican wave.'

Hyam knows the downside of football routines which he says can induce fatigue as well a severe bout of the fidgets. 'It can be quite upsetting if I miss just one part of my routine or forget to check how many times I've done something.' After years of keeping to his checks and balances he founded Checkers Incognito where supporters of any football club can walk in at any time of day or night to talk about their problems using a false identity and fake occupation. Apart from

Hyam, who's become too famous for his own good. Members meet regularly when it is important to arrive late so as not to seem over keen. Then they join the rest and sit blindfold on a purple and green mat, Chunter United's original colours.

'Hello I'm Hyam I am and I'm an over keen football supporter and registered checker and chunterer.'

'Hi everyone, my false name's Knobbly Knees and I'm over keen as well. I began getting the football jitters because I was afraid my team were going to lose whilst I was at work as a prune picker. There was a buzz to begin with but I found I needed to consume more and more prunes and information. Instead of working I hid on the loo looking up facts and figures on my phone. Eventually I got the sack.'

'I'm Plankton but it's not my real name that's Gerald…Oops!… I can't resist counting my collection of ticket stubs over and over again. I'm an accountant but I've been diagnosed with Losing Count Syndrome.'

'Me too' crept in Treecreeper who said that she found it confusing dividing the time when she wasn't madly following football between being a dog walker called Curls and a mobile hairdresser called Spot.

'Hi, I'm Art Deco. I'm known as Deco the Gekko because I breed lizards. I find that if I don't decorate their cage to keep me busy I worry that the stadium needs a once over.'

'Hello, Sandra here. I'm a part-time window cleaner with MI5 and one of the few people who can tidy the grass on a football field under-cover whilst snipping away at it with a pair of nail scissors. I listen in to boardroom chatter on a long-handled pogo stick. First I say "Hello" to each corner flag so they think I'm just a nutter.'

Many are the tales of fans whose lives have been wrecked by checking and chuntering. Indeed, this is why Hyam set up Checkers Incognito which also led to him being voted Superfan of the Year three years running. On the last occasion he was presented with a jetpack by Colonel Mustard who said he was keen as mustard to do this so Hyam could expand the scope of his checking and chuntering. This Hyam has done with S for Superfan pinned to his chest handing out leaflets and helping distribute parachute payments to clubs relegated after points were deducted following checks on their finances.

Hyam Keenbritches no longer charges his electric bike from a lamp post but his jetpack instead. He has accepted many an invitation to demonstrate his gyratory skills as a form of half-time entertainment. Fans delight at the sight of him looming out of the sky like an apparition at their football grounds bent on rescuing some poor soul who's given in under the strain of being over keen. He lives quietly on a nondescript estate in Lower Chunter where a neighbour told reporters he's something of a recluse. 'Except when training in his back garden on a flight simulator'. There is currently a move to rename the Worthless Insurance Policy Stadium the Keenbritches Arena. Provided everything checks out.

Superfan Hyam Keenbritches now travels to games by jetpack.

Play resumes ...

30 minutes

At Huddersfield, a host of young hopefuls played one match with 20 or more players a side. The whole game was odd. We rotated in blocks of five, ten minutes at a time. It meant that there were up to 30 players on the pitch at any given moment because Spud, the guy in charge, wasn't keeping a proper tab.[1] As soon as you got going he would blow his whistle and off you came. Ten minutes later, or whenever he felt like it, Spud would sound it three times and shout, 'On you go, you with the pudding basin haircut ... Left back position,' even if you normally played up front on the right.

Each team had a queue of goalkeepers who took it in turns to step onto the goal line. Somehow, they had spewed out invitations to everyone on their 'watch list'. Worse still, everyone turned up thinking they were the object of the exercise, that the others were there to make up the numbers. There's a lot of psyching out in football and that day was no different, 'I'm only here because I'm not needed at Turf Moor.' 'Weren't you rejected by Peterborough United?' You believe what you want to believe in football and it's a good idea to think twice before taking something as the gospel truth. I was only there because I took every chance I could get to join the ranks of the professionals.

Swarming like bees in a forward line of nine may sound interesting but for the players it was confusing. Strikers and defenders on the same side began fighting each other for the ball, or keeping it to themselves so that there were several games within the main game going on all at the same time. Everyone wanted to score, no-one wanted to go home without being noticed. We played in a rickety

---

1. All clubs have someone called Spud or Bindy somewhere along the chain of command. Managers only attend trials if wheeled on to say 'Hi'.

old stadium on the moors. It chucked it down and to make matters worse both teams wore the same blue and white striped, hand-me-down, now thoroughly sodden, shirts that the senior professionals had done with. But only after untangling them from a huge basket. We just wore different coloured bibs, the kind kids do when making mud pies. There was lot of mud that day.

At half-time Spud called everyone together and pointed upwards. 'See that hill with the TV transmitter on top? Right, off you go. Three times around it following the buzz of the radio waves, twice up and down Yorkshire Sculpture Park[2] leapfrogging the Henry Moores and jumping through the hole in a Barbara Hepworth. No stopping for a cuppa in one of them Clarice Cliff mugs they've got on show. Back here in 15 minutes. No short cuts.'

They did sign up one guy, someone I knew well, and I could have told them straightaway he wouldn't make it. He didn't. I should have been a football scout.

The real nail in my Huddersfield Town coffin was a 16-year-old wunderkind called Dennis Law who they'd just signed and who played in the same position. Law went on to captain Scotland and play for Manchester City, Torino, Manchester United and then Manchester City again. A once-in-a-generation player, he kept me out of the team. That's my story and I'm sticking to it. When I became a lawyer I learned all about the importance of sticking to the same tale, avoiding *ex post facto* rationalisation[3] and having a good story to begin with.

---

2. Then Bretton Hall College of Education where we spent many pleasant evenings with those training to be teachers.
3. Cart before horse explanation after the outcome is known.

A Case of Mistaken Identity

There was a long-serving defender with the same name as myself at Huddersfield Town. Only that Brian Gibson spelt his name like the snail on the *Magic Roundabout*. It didn't score me any points and I don't think their lack of overtures in my direction was due to his name having a vowel in the middle. I did get asked if I was 'Brian's lad' but that was it. Maybe I should have taken a flier and said yes because he was popular with the fans. When Brian's playing days ended he worked in a dripping factory. Someone has to do it and I shouldn't make fun of dripping, especially having been called Streaky in Hull. I'm sure his employers valued the public relations aspect that many ex-footballers bring to non-football undertakings.

40 minutes

In defeat I trudged back once more to Barnsley where I lost enthusiasm for the game for a time. Back then there weren't any reality TV shows like BBC 1's *Boot Dreams: Now or Never* (which started to air as I was finishing this book). Reality shows usually involve telling contestants, 'You're leaving us today!' or 'You're fired!' *Boot Dreams* breaks the mould by aiming to rescue football rejects who train together and play as a team of their own, only eliminating those who truly can't hack it. A bit like The Outcasts in one of my stories. I notice quite a few of those taking part were making the most of their tales of the clubs they were at before their services were dispensed with.

When I'd recovered from the disappointment I dropped down a good way and played for my local team, Pogmoor Panthers. If you say it quickly in a high wind with a large pebble in your mouth it sounds like 'Paris Saint-Germain' the top French outfit. We were good at pretending to be something we weren't, as you'll see, and I should really say that I played for Pogmoor Panthers and England. This happened in unusual circumstances. A youth team from behind the Iron Curtain was on an exchange visit and their itinerary included a stopover in the People's Republic of South Yorkshire. The visitors had been promised a game against an England side. The problem was no-one had made any preparations. At the eleventh hour our manager got a call from 'an official' asking if we could help smooth over international relations.

'We've tried every other team and they're in hiding. What about your lot? ... Poggie, are they available by chance. It could earn you friends in the east.'

'You bet,' replied our manager, 'East is east and the Potted North is west so we'll see you on the northern edge of the south of town on Saturday.'

'No betting, no fun, no games, and keep a straight face ... The mayor's coming ... wear something muted, grey preferably ... that doesn't stain easily. There's a reception at the Queen's Hotel afterwards. It's likely to involve beetroot soup.'

'Do we need vetting?' 'No, Vetting's playing for them ... and by the way every member of the team will need to sign the Official Secrets Act, so tell 'em to arrive early.'

I'm only kidding about the Act and Vetting wasn't on the team sheet either. I made him up.

With that I imagine the 'official' took off his dark glasses and went back to his day job as a rivet inspector. All very hush hush. At the ground we were handed our England kits and asked to keep the arrangements quiet. We won but the venue and even the score remain classified. One of the best kept secrets of the Cold War is that we weren't the eleven the Soviets had been promised.

England v USSR (Top Secret).

Sparrow Grass and Thespian Royalty

At the Queen's Hotel it was the first time I'd been in the upstairs dining room and my first encounter with sparrow grass. That's what I thought the waiter said when he asked, 'Asparagus, sir?'. I'd seen liquorice which grew like topsy in Pontefract and looked similar, but that delicacy was a lot more chewy. I learned that you dip it in melted butter. Asparagus that is, not liquorice.

Elsie Tanner of *Coronation Street* was there because she'd been opening a shop that afternoon. Or rather Pat Phoenix, the actress who played her, who'd been invited to Barnsley because her names both began with P. After winks and nods she glided over and started chatting, having mistaken us for the celebrities we weren't. She leaned over and asked, 'What've you been up to my dears?' Thinking she meant generally rather than that afternoon I replied that we'd been to Sheffield the previous evening to see the Beatles. 'Oh, how are the boys?' the soap star asked as if she was their mother and hadn't seen them for a couple of weeks.

THE REF HAS A FINGER TO HIS EAR. Yes, it's a check for a possible penalty. Or was there an offside in the build up? Then again, did the ball come off a defender's ear just before it hit the forward's arm and then grazed the centre back's little finger? There's a lot to unravel here, and it could take a while, especially as this league's experimental VAR system depends on viewing the phone footage of every fan in the stadium...

Tall Tale No. 3
Old Soss

Football has many unsung heroes. Third team players, back room or admin staff, ball boys and girls. Folk who if not recorded disappear faster than the vanishing foam referees use to mark out where to take a free kick from. Like little Jack Horner the kit man in the corner and Penny Black from the post room. Not to mention rejects such as Mark Marker who was so bad at marking opponents he didn't leave a mark, or Eddie Foot who left to become a chiropodist. 'Game management, game management,' Eddie was heard to remark, 'I'd rather manage bunions.' All long forgotten. Consigned to the Great Sports Bin of Football History.

'Old Soss' was the nickname of Dan Treacle. 'My parents were called Treacle,' he once explained, 'but it sticks in the gullet.' Treacle played for six leading clubs in a career spanning 15 weeks so keen was each club to offload him to the next. He then uttered the immortal words 'I think it's all over' and went into management. Determined never to be sacked again, he set up his own team where he single-handedly built the stadium with his bare hands. Originally known as The Pig's Ear that famous ground became known as Paradise Park and the team he created Outcasts United.

When Old Soss celebrated his tenth year in charge admirers paid tribute to his life and work. 'Treacle is one of a kind and a gentleman … even if he dresses like a tramp' reported Wendy Warbles on Radio Water Bottle. 'Except on match days,' added Outcast Ladies' captain Gladys Gone. 'When he wears a Fedora … or is that the Italian chap he signed on loan?'

'Soss is an innovator,' butted in Outcast's right-winger, Stan Butting who had a habit of jutting out his head when he approached people. 'Vertigo, vertigo, vertigo!' the supporters would shout as opponents were left dizzy on the floor. 'He was the first to introduce autograph breaks and to try using a backwards facing forward line.'

'Why do they call him Soss?' asked Wendy.

'It's a mystery,' chipped in Willy Tonks. Tonks spent the week teaching the players to chip the ball in so felt comfortable with the tactic. 'Some folks say it stands for S-O-S, a cry for help, others that Soss rhymes with boss … or that it stands for sozzled … or for sausage even. Then after a long pause indicative of too much heading of the ball Tonks added, 'German sausage. Old Soss loved Bratwurst, especially after The Outcasts toured Bavaria.'

Wendy Warble's listeners were also to hear that Soss was proud of his watch, always trying to get it to add or subtract minutes at the end of games depending on who was winning. If this failed, he would go out and buy a new one. 'I never understood that,' continued Tonks, 'but then I went straight from junior school to The Outcasts' Academy and it was downhill every day after that.'

'Didn't you learn anything?' warbled Wendy Warbles.

'They taught me about dribbling, ducking, diving and how to play without the ball … and I've been told I've an intelligent left foot,' replied Tonks. 'With any luck I'll become a legend like Old Soss.'

Soss was indeed a legend. Especially at Paradise Park where he was founder, chair, manager, assistant manager, coach, scout, medic, stretcher bearer, groundsman, programme seller, electrician and security guard. He also cleaned the players' boots, washed the kit and swept the terraces. None of this was unusual for Soss who, ever energetic, also worked as a time and motion expert when he found the time or the motion. Eventually to ease his burden The Outcasts took on an apprentice. 'I've decided we should become a feeder team,' he announced. No-one ever did find out who or what The Outcasts were going to feed but it sounded good as did talk of scaling the football pyramid. 'We're going to be big in Egypt,' the apprentice was assured as he signed a no-Cairo-no-pay agreement. 'Until then you're in Paradise … Here, fix this picture of The Sphinx to your shirt. You can start by cleaning the toilets.'

Handyman supreme and ambitious beyond self-belief, Soss was hands-on at his 'Theatre of Nightmares' which he built on common land without planning permission before painting it Outcast Orange. It stood like the setting sun in a deep valley, a mound of granite at each corner on which Soss planned to build four matching hotels. 'For the prince and his retinue,' he declared, 'the one who's going to buy the club.' Paradise Park attracted anything up to 50,000 spectators on a good day, but mostly outside the ground looking in from the surrounding hills where they got a panoramic view. The largest official crowd stands at 773.

Build it and add bits here and there was his mantra as he set about the task using plywood off-cuts, rusty corrugated sheets and clumps of meadow grass looted from neighbouring fields in the depth of night. Next, he stuck signs on nearby roads next to the official ones saying 'You Are Now Entering Bandit Country'. 'Paradise Park This Way … Mind the Pips' as the club's nickname became. 'Last warning,' said the local magistrates. 'Next time you add an unlicensed sign you'll be wearing an orange jumpsuit and we'll be squeezing your pips.'

During the playing season the mangled turf was left uncut until it was ten inches deep, enough to bring on cramp within minutes in visiting teams who weren't used to it. The goal nets were made from recycled carrot sacks sewn together in batches of 100. 'Outcast Orange, why not?' Soss would challenge his critics. The stadium was entirely off-grid. Not to be outdone Soss brought in a shed load of candles which were placed in jam jars mounted on upturned oil drums. Hoping that the last candle would not burn out before the process needed to start all over again, he re-lived his days as a milkman running up and down the gangways swapping old for new and striking a match just in time. Later he installed a pedal bike linked to a generator to power the floodlights. In the winter when the below sea level pitch turned to sludge he tipped sand everywhere and gave the players quad bikes to navigate the dunes.

One challenge for teams unfamiliar with Paradise Park was the row of elm trees that stood at the left-hand corner of the six-yard-box at the Canal End. These had to be negotiated as if they were a flat back seven. Refusing to cut them down on the grounds that players needed the oxygen, Soss famously quipped, 'So long as the players change ends it's even Stevens'. Confusingly, Evan Stevens played inside right and Steven Evans for the reserves. What Soss had really meant to say was, 'It's a game of two halves'. In due course he moved the trees along the valley, a mammoth task surpassed only by the time he diverted the canal to square off the opposite corner.

Rather than splash out on such niceties as a fence, in the early days Soss cordoned off Paradise Park using crime scene tape and old bed-steads. His rickety grandstand swayed in the breeze and bore a sign saying 'Temporary Capacity 19.' He printed programmes on an old duplicator but that really didn't set the right tone.

On days when referees were late or they'd been kidnapped by Out-cast Security, Soss would grab a whistle, put a spare set of eyes in the back of his head and oversee matches. But only on days when he wasn't standing in for the club mascot Crunchy in an outfit made from old cereal packets. If there wasn't a match he'd organize boxing tournaments, Wall of Death motorcycle stunts or concerts starring a kazoo band he fronted whose song *Darling Leave the Second Ball to Me* became the most downloaded track by an over-optimistic football club chairman of all time. 'Diversify or evaporate' he'd tell folk as he got up a head of steam and spread himself too thinly.

Most of his team lived in the same postcode area as he did and called him Uncle. But he was planning to take The Outcasts 'all the way there' and as critics suggested 'all the way back'. Nothing but nothing deterred him from his dream. Other than an outdated pair of spectacles and lack of sensible restraint. That's how he came to sign Noddy Normous and Sam Bitesize. He of the square head and she of the lethal left boot. Oh, and Pam Spam ('Spam Fritter' as she was known) making up the Pam and Sam of his famous 'Mix and Match Now You See Me Now You Don't' experiment. As Radio Water Bottle reported 'Pam and Sam were followed by an audacious attempt to sign Betty Skyrocket who was already a legend in her own backyard. But apart from a couple of trial games her career did not suffer from his grandiose ideas.' One proud protégé, Charlie Gunn, a former circus performer with a large red nose, was a crowd-pleasing super-sub who Soss fired onto the pitch using a cannon that he'd retrieved from a neighbour's pond while scuba diving for old timber to build a shed for the club tractor. 'Like a tomato out of a trap,' Soss described it.

The team trained in the evenings. Except on Thursdays as that was the day Soss put on a wet suit to reclaim balls from the canal. 'So they can dry out by match day,' he explained. It is said that the players lived on raw sardines and saltwater before big matches. He encouraged them to commit offences serious enough to merit short prison sentences. 'You'll be more eager when you come out,' he would tell them. 'They're all blooming criminals anyway' he'd been advised by one referee. 'What happens in the dressing room stays in the dressing room,' he replied.

In their final game before the bulldozers appeared on the horizon, The Outcasts lost 12-1, which Soss attributed to a need to defend. It would have been 13-1 but for a kink in the crossbar, the result of a botched repair after Stan Butting banged his head against it. Soss celebrated the one goal The Outcasts did score by taking the team for a three-week break to the South Seas where they played a local side using a beach ball losing 6-5. 'Below expectations,' Soss admitted. The club's lack of glory was symbolised by a homemade flag that fluttered over the entrance to Paradise Park to its dying day. 'We parked the bus so often the engine seized up,' said Soss.

Many are the stories told and retold about Old Soss. But he is nowhere to be found in the record books. No trace of Paradise Park exists. A local woman who wished to remain anonymous said the council arrived with the bailiffs and a fleet of trucks and hauled it away. And that Soss, who suffers bouts of euphoria, now lives in a home where he paints white lines on the grass and re-positions the garden gnomes muttering 'Keep it tight … game management, head for the corner flag … The other side can't score when you've got the ball!' Another local claimed he was being held by police after becoming a burglar in pursuit of the medals and silverware he never won.

There are those who say that Paradise Park never existed. This despite a photograph reproduced in *Lost Stadiums of Football History* which shows the ground in its hey-day. 'A forgery, you can't trust anything these days,' say disbelievers. I know they must be wrong as ephemera sometimes turn up at jungle flea markets and car boot sales.

Old Soss erected signs to his DIY stadium.

Play resumes …

43 minutes

Pogmoor Panthers may have been the first team to field a young woman. Hannah McTavish played alongside her two brothers. She was one of the fastest, trickiest wingers to grace a football field. Hannah travelled down the wing as if riding a 2,000 cc Harley-Davidson motorcycle, or perhaps a 125 cc BSA Bantam was more likely as news that America or anywhere else more than a few miles distant existed had not yet filtered through to many people in the Potted North. Her father had played for Glasgow club Celtic. She should have been celebrated as say the Lauren James or Chloe Kelly of her day, or being Scottish, Aston Villa and Scotland's Rachel Corsie.

I'm pretty sure we were also one of the first teams to field a black player. Emmanuel popped up in our class at school when his family arrived from Nigeria. 'Manny' had the fastest legs ever fitted and he mesmerised defenders. As brilliant as he was cheerful, several clubs had eyes on him. Like many young players his priorities changed once he had responsibilities.

We once played two games on the same day, losing the first 6-5 and winning the second 12-1. I often think of that feat when I hear highly paid modern-day players moaning about having to perform in too many matches. Also, when I listen to the manager of a losing side rebuffing the media with, 'We're not looking back, we're focusing on the next game.' 'But not one that same afternoon,' I'm tempted to say. I'd have been happy to play a third game in the evening but no team came forward.

The Panthers' modern-day incarnation, community-driven AFC Pogmoor,[1] fields several women's and girls' teams, so I think they've

---

1. See https://www.afcpogmoor.co.uk

continued in the pioneering tradition we began with Hannah McTavish all those years ago.

Maybe we should have been called Pogmoor Copycats. Nowadays, at least in junior football and even with middle-ranking sides it seems fairly commonplace to add a tag but not then. The pace-setters were a club on the far side of town called Athersley Tigers, a district that has since forged a name for itself with Athersley Recreation who play in the Northern Counties East Football League and have done pretty well in the FA Cup.

Uncle Jeremiah's Bodyguard Service

Across town the other way I see Lundwood is according to Zoopla, 'A desirable area'. Back then it was bandit country. We were fortunate because Uncle Jeremiah, the one who sold dud footballs in Leeds, had moved his empire there and hired out bodyguards. His sons were heavyweight boxers. One day I was hit square in the face by a punch from a gloved hand as one of them opened the front door to me. 'Hardening up', Uncle Jerry called it.

I'm told Norman Hunter, the notorious Leeds United and England hard man, who played for and managed Barnsley, declined all invitations to go for a drink in Lundwood as he was concerned about the police going around six at a time holding hands. Perhaps he shouldn't have worried. Bert Tindill (who I mention later) kept the Lundwood Hotel[2] when his playing days were over and it seems they loved ex-players. Brian Glover the fearsome 'Leon Arras the Man from Paris' (again see later) once lived there amongst the tough nuts of those days.

---

2.   I believe it was this now lost premises.

Peep peep!
Half time

Another football-themed thespian tale comes from my days as a trustee of our local theatre in Jane Austin Country, The Haymarket in Basingstoke. The place is also home to Basingstoke Town of the Southern League Premier Division South, who over 30 years ago reached the Second Round of the FA Cup before being beaten 3-2 by Torquay United. The following season they reached the First Round and beat Wycombe Wanderers 5-4 on penalties after a 2-2 draw to force a replay, before a Camrose Ground crowd of 5,085, a record for a home match. After that they took Northampton Town to a replay, losing 4-3 on penalties. They reached the First Round again soon afterwards to lose just 2-1 against AFC Bournemouth who were then in the old Second Division. Their two existing nicknames are 'The Stokes' and 'The Dragons'. I suggest a third might be 'The Doughnuts' after Doughnut City, Basingstoke's other monicker, because the town is surrounded by umpteen roundabouts. Visitors say it looks like Dallas in the USA so maybe they should join that country's Major League Soccer (MLS) and play David Beckham's Inter Miami. Remember to book tickets early.

For a time in Hampshire we did 'theatre digs' along the lines of Jim and Jenny my landlords in Hull who lost out on the football pools. One thespian who came to stay was John Forgeham. John played the manager of Earls Park FC in the award winning TV series *Footballers' Wives*. His character Frank Laslett was the polar opposite of Hull City manager the kindly Cliff Britton. John appeared in many well-known productions, including alongside Michael Caine in *The Italian Job*. 'Michael Caine's my best friend,' John would remind us most days and we'd dutifully answer, 'Not many people know that.'

You get used to things like this with actors, as you do the notion that every play is about to transfer to London's West End or go on tour. The way every football club is set for great things. Some do of course, just like some football clubs win the trophy they promised everyone they would, but it doesn't take long to realise only one team can or that few theatrical productions hit the heights. *Dear England*, James Graham's drama based on England manager Gareth Southgate's mission to avenge his missed penalty kick in a semi-final of the World Cup and tackle masculinity issues in football has defied the odds. As this book went to press it had just opened to sell out audiences at the National Theatre, with Joseph Fiennes as Southgate. Make that one up!

It's a man's game...

Southgate's attempts to change football prompt me to mention a bit more about the women's game. As many places do, my adopted home town has a thriving women's club (independently of Barnsley FC). It plays at senior and junior levels. There is an Emerging Talent Centre and plans for a new £5 million stadium. Hannah McTavish, my Pogmoor Panthers team mate (above), would have been proud, as would my fictional creation Betty Skyrocket and her friends who all say they would have loved to play for Barnsley Women but that no-one asked. England Women's Bethany England of Tottenham Hotspur FC Women, formerly of Doncaster Belles, Liverpool and Chelsea, was born in Barnsley. She became Women's Super League Player of the Year among other accolades. Women's football is on an exponential rise.

GOODNESS THEY SEEM TO HAVE BEEN PLAYING with one of Uncle Jeremiah's dud footballs because this one's gone flat as a pancake. This is not a club that can afford to buy more than one ball at a time so there's been a whip round and the ref has sent the fourth official to the retail park along the road for another. I need to hold fire...

Tall Tale No. 4
The Goalkeepers' Convention

oalkeeping is a funny business. 'You have to be a bit loose in the arms and legs and not averse to a few knocks to the vital parts,' mused Albert Flapper, legend of the sticks, as he began his address to the Annual Convention of the Goalkeepers' Union. Everything was being filmed for the now infamous fly-on-the-wall documentary *Life Between the Goalposts* that never aired because of what I will tell you here. The police are still investigating what turned out to be the very last time such shenanigans were allowed and the insurers remain in dispute with the organizers. 'Who in their right mind would let footballers onto their premises in the first place?' argue the loss adjusters. Since the case has not yet reached the highest court in the land I've been told that as a prospective witness I may disclose the bare facts, only the bare facts and nothing but the bare facts.

'Who'd be a goalkeeper?' Flapper continued. His words echoing across the conference room as several hundred delegates watched videos of *The Greatest Saves of All Time* on their mobile phones. Before the event was banned, every goalie worth his Dragon Grease attended. This time the Hotel Grinding House had prepared for it by raising its ceilings and borrowing items from the Extra Long Bed Company. A goal net fluttered from the flagpole, the waiters wore shin pads, the pub across the road was re-named *The Flying Squirrel,* and the hotel's optional restaurant for those tired of everyday hotel fare had been decked out with real grass and white painted lines, except around the most trafficked parts which were pure mud, so as to make the keepers feel at home. Experts attended to give talks and the delegates carried towels and sipped from water bottles which they rolled inside their hats and tucked behind any available column as they paced back and forth in the foyer. 'Nerves,' someone said, 'Habit, routine, auto-pilot…every six yards a space to be defended, every pillar, chair or waste paper bin a goalpost.'

'Make sure they've got clean sheets,' demanded the hotel manager who'd seen it all before. Get them laundered twice over…Tell them they can take them home afterwards. They like to keep clean sheets.'

On the Tuesday, Sir Ben Bong, seasoned international and Keeper of the Year, gave a talk entitled The Art of Playing Out from the Back. This had been eagerly awaited by those delegates who'd made the mistake of thinking opposing forwards couldn't do a high press. Afterwards some of those in attendance were seen on the hotel lawn pretending geraniums were full backs and daisies opposing forwards. 'Weed, there's a weed behind you!' yelled a spectator from one of the raised beds.

Wednesday was Punching Out the Ball Day when Naomi Fitz-Nicely, Professor of Arms and Legs at Long Forgotten University, addressed the players accompanied by demonstrations from a ballerina and a heavyweight boxer. Later there was a trip on the hotel lake before breaking into groups to discuss Catching a Greasy Ball or Pretending to be Busy When the Ball is at the Other End (choice to be notified in advance). Then on Thursday, after an overlong discussion about Time Wasting the day was free to squander. Until the Grand Dinner in the evening. Just in time to sober-up by the weekend.

The Goalkeepers' Union has a hierarchy. Full Members must have played at least once in goal. Associate members are those who've only sat on the bench, such as Arnold Squatter, who was a substitute for five years without being called upon to enter the field of play. The one time he did get close he was fast asleep. 'They didn't wake me as by that time the guy on the field had recovered,' he said. 'Money for old rope, if you ask me, I am so lacking in game time that every time I catch the ball it slips out of my fingers.' Associate members cannot vote except by mistake. There is a Wannabe Section for those still dreaming of a life between the posts, a Lady Keepers' Section and splinter groups for LGBTQI+ keepers, foreigners and those from unfathomable backgrounds. 'Diversity doesn't just mean different styles of catching a ball,' commented the union's public relations guru. 'No goalkeeper is an island' it said on his t-shirt.

During Sir Ben Bong's Playing Out from the Back session he explained that the idea is to draw the opposition forwards, so a sudden long ball out will fox their depleted back line. 'The important thing is not to stumble over the ball whilst doing this,' said Sir Ben, caressing an imaginary football with his toes before falling flat on his backside. The aim is to trick the other team about when an attack will be launched. 'Think of it as hoovering up the other side's players … sucking the lifeblood out of them … then emptying the bag over their heads.'

'Kick the ball back and forth, like bagatelle or ping-pong,' yelled out Peter Dismal, long-serving stalwart of Pincushion Town, well-known for making strange interjections. 'Back in your six yard box,' said the chair. 'Bing, bong, ping, pong,' answered Dismal who although he could be infuriating was tolerated having sponsored the Dismal Performance Medal. Sir Ben showed a video clip that he thought was from a recent match before commenting, 'Sorry folks, that's me and my partner on holiday.' It was unlike him to make such a mistake because he'd attended so many courses on How to Keep Your Audience Awake that he rarely got it wrong. 'Great football nation that,' he announced hoping to make it look as if it was part of what he'd intended.

Most popular was a seminar on Psyching Out Penalty-Takers which attracted 237 participants as against a total of five across the other topics combined. There would have been 238 but Dido Skiver of Gooseberry Preserves Reserves had slipped out to practice skydiving after asking loud and highly memorable questions from the floor. This in the hope he'd not be missed after he absconded. Everyone would think he was still there keeping a low profile, a trick he'd learnt from a college friend who was an illusionist. On one occasion everyone copied his ploy and the speaker faced an empty hall. Skiver later wrote a book in which he described how he'd tried to apply the art of disappearing to the game itself but had concluded the only way not to be seen by opponents was to get sent off.

'It's not just about staring out the penalty-taker' said Owen Gole, the group leader. 'Who of you wants to share other methods?'

The avalanche started:

'Water bottle: spin it, toss it up and down.'

'Swing from the crossbar.'

'Read a newspaper.'

'Face the other way and bend over.'

'Pace furiously back and forth.'

'Hide behind the goalpost.'

'Whisper "I wonder what your other half's up to."'

After much disagreement the group decided that the main thing was to unsettle a penalty-taker's brain solids. The group's elected note taker Paddy Jotter wrote this down for his upcoming report in *The Save*.

It turned out there were no limits to goalkeeping wiles at penalty time. There was even a suggestion that goalkeepers should use algorithms. 'Artificial intelligence. I keep a tiny device in my sock linked to a computer. This works out for me the entire history of the penalty-taker, cross-matches it with every save I've ever made and calculates where the ball will end up. It then delivers an undetectable impulse that causes me to dive the right way.'

'We must all learn to live with technology,' said Owen Gole in a bid to show that he knew more than his charges. 'The truth is,' he added, 'it's not your ordinary penalty that matters ... it's those in the shoot-out.' As he mentioned these words dark descended. It was as if the apocalypse had begun. Mature goalkeepers hid under their seats whilst novices cried, 'Help Mum!'

'Every goalkeeper's nightmare,' someone shouted from beneath the carpet.

'Sudden death' another moaned as he ran into the kitchen.

'I'd rather put my head in a cauldron of soup.' This from a huge chap capable of holding a football in the palm of each hand.

Some goalkeepers are never the same after a penalty shoot-out.

When Thursday evening came everyone swapped their tracksuits for posh clobber. A group of admirers had gathered for pre-dinner drinks in *The Flying Squirrel*. 'Goalkeeping's a vocation,' explained Albert Flapper, reminiscing about his years with Minster Monsters. 'Some kids get into it because they are last one standing after a round of "eeny, meeny, miny, moe" but others take to it naturally ... They wake up one morning shouting "Goalie ... goalie ... I've got to be a goalie" ... Big kids, small kids, every size of kid ... Shall we return to the hotel and find a table?'

Dinner was a rowdy affair. Goalkeepers are rarely seen in formal dress and many only know what life is about once they don a goalkeeping jersey and head for the pitch. Or go up the pitch when desperation sets in during the closing seconds. 'A goalie thrusting forwards on 93 minutes is a fish out of water,' remarked Peter Dismal, 'but in the dying embers of the last minute when the referee is on a trip of his or her own it's not over until he or she blows the whistle.' Dismal was famous for his outbursts but they sometimes contained microscopic insights. 'I don't know much about nothing,' he said. 'Nothing about knives and forks, even less about duck in orange sauce,' he confessed glancing at the menu, 'but I've heard of duck. Duck and the ball's in the goal. Don't duck and who knows where it might end up?'

As anyone who has spent more than three seconds in the company of professional footballers will tell you they talk of little else but the game. The next game, the last game, the game after the game before last. Who's signed where, who's on loan and, amongst goalkeepers, who's played a howler. Likewise mistakes of etiquette, though not inevitable, occur as frequently as a misjudged back pass. 'Mine, mine, yours, get shot ... right, left, pass, pass, here, to me ... Pass the salt please ... Who's marking the vinaigrette,' muttered Dismal.

Picture the scene in the fading light as the evening drew to a close. Bow ties loosened, belts undone, chests bared and furniture all over the place. Hundreds of arms making octopus-style goalkeeping gestures as imaginary footballs were saved and spare bread rolls tossed over people's heads like long range missiles into the far top corner. All accompanied by sideways leaps, football chants and the expletives of an unruly mob. Wham! It wasn't long before chaos erupted.

Wally Buffet, ex-international referee, looked contorted. Standing by a trolley helping himself whilst pretending to examine someone's studs he was also chuckling to himself trying to work out where best to do this so that he could see his reflection into infinity in the room's enormous mirrors. Interrupted by the melee, he added to this complex manoeuvre by brandishing red cards, yellow cards and first aid kits. Not that anyone took the slightest notice.

Before long the walls caved in, the ceiling crashed to the ground and the fire brigade arrived, just as burning candles met the display of jerseys strung out on a washing line across the stage. To this day it is unclear why the Hotel Grinding House was completely trashed. That weekend spectators at grounds around the country who had not yet heard the news were left wondering why goalkeepers sported singed eyebrows, no hair and the odd sling.

Albert Flapper is not forgotten. He plays in the lower leagues and has confessed to deliberately letting in the occasional goal. 'I'd be out of a job if we ever got promoted,' he once confided. Sir Bob Bong is no longer the iconic figure he once was after succumbing to a rare colour-related sense of anxiety that kicks in whenever he sees red, white, black, yellow, green, blue or for that matter any other colour of football shirt. Professor Fitz-Nicely has become head of Sports Science at Long Forgotten University, whilst Arnold Squatter, he of the slippery fingers, is still searching for the Golf Trophy that he dropped into the hotel fish tank. The Dismal Performance Medal is now known as the Nutmeg Award. As for Dido Skiver, he's completely vanished.

As this book went to press it was being reported that all attempts to reach a settlement between the umpteen parties involved in these events had failed. That the Duff Transactions Squad were inquiring into what happened to the proceeds of the raffle. Two items are on public view at the Museum of the Six Yard Box: the dentures Owen Gole damaged showing delegates how to catch a football with their teeth and the trapeze that an aerobatics troupe used to demonstrate how to make a flying save. What remains of Hotel Grinding House is being held in an unidentified warehouse behind a flat back four of armed guards.

Few people know why the Hotel Grinding
House was completely trashed.

Play resumes . . .

45 minutes

To my parents' despair I was becoming a football layabout. I didn't even have the wherewithal to be a 'ten bob millionaire'[1] which is what we called those who talked like they owned the world when they called round on the scrounge. I was however familiar with the way to the Town Hall and Ms Pinkerton was a shoulder to cry on.

'Third time lucky,' I thought as she rummaged yet again. 'How about becoming a legal eagle?' she asked, playing her latest card. Somehow it didn't register that she meant become a lawyer rather than pop down to London for a trial with The Eagles at Crystal Palace.

After a few seconds reality hit as I went numb and my hopes of becoming a professional footballer started to fade. Years on and apart from wistful trips to Selhurst Park (and many other football grounds) as one of tens of thousands of onlookers I'm left to rue what might have been. To grind my teeth over the fact that I became a round peg in a square hole. Though even that had its weird side when years on, having long since abandoned my Football Career that Never Was, I played in The Game that Never Was.

This happened during a legal gathering in Cardiff. We agreed (as you do of a balmy, or is it 'barmy', evening) in the conference bar, to play next day, 7 am kick-off, before breakfast. The match was to take place in the grounds of Cardiff Castle, North versus South. Only two players turned up. Both northerners. One of us agreed to transfer to the South in their absence and we went ahead as scheduled, one-a-side, hoofing the ball around on a strip of grass between the castle walls and a public footpath. It was on a slant reminiscent of Yeovil Town's old 'sloping ground', the Huish Athletic Stadium, where often

---

1. Fifty pence millionaire doesn't quite have the same ring to it.

as giant killers they confounded so many visiting teams over the years.[2] We then conspired to submit a report saying the match had ended in a 3-3 draw. It was duly published in a much-vaunted law journal. The other chap went on to become a Crown Court judge having airbrushed the event from his curriculum vitae.[3]

55 minutes

Back in my earliest football days there was Sandy Soot, chimney sweep, who said he'd been a sweeper of a different kind with several 'big clubs'. He'd come home in the evening to the houses by the rough, stony pitch on which we practiced. He suddenly arrived on the scene from nowhere. After wiping off the dirt he'd join us for a kick about. He had a shock of bright red hair, receding on top, and would race around like a five year old. He didn't seem to have any connection to the area and for all I know could have just been released from prison or was on the run. Sandy took on an unsolicited coaching role and taught us how to take a penalty.

'Lesson one, *decide early what you're going to do ... Never, ever* change your mind ... Lesson two, it's best to *hit the ball low and straight for the inside of one of the uprights...* Lesson three, if you *kick the ball hard enough no goalkeeper in the world is going to get to it.*' Provided the goalkeeper stays on the goal line, as he or she should, this I believe is a scientific fact unknown to many spot kick takers.

We practiced until we could score every time. I don't think I ever missed a penalty after that, including those I struck past the legendary Harry Hough who, after he quit playing some 350 times for Barnsley, took a job as player-manager of Denaby United. That's where I helped

---

2. A pattern I believe was first set in 1949 when still members of the lowly Southern League, Yeovil beat then First Division (Premier League level) Sunderland 2-1, who that same year only missed out on being champions by one point and goal difference. Quite a win!

3. This is the first time I've made this public so I risk being disbarred.

him to paint the white lines. It's hard to think of this one time talisman, who only missed playing for England due to breaking his arm, mixing whitewash in a bucket, marking out the pitch and spreading sand in the goalmouth, but he did.

Harry Hough was right hand man to TV personality and Brentford then Fulham player, and later Coventry City manager, Jimmy Hill. Hill chaired the Professional Footballer's Association with Harry by his side. Harry Hough glistened from some lubricant on the football field as users of Dragon Grease do in this book.

Like many lost souls, Sandy Soot disappeared in a puff of cigarette smoke (which is also how I remember him arriving and playing). He was like a big kid who if he hit the deck bounced like a toddler. I learned to do that from him as well and it's served me well over the years. Maybe he was sent down to Earth with the sole mission of teaching us how to take penalties. 'Job done' he was whisked back by the Head Penalty Angel. It's real life tales like these that encouraged me to write this book. Nothing could be stranger than some things that actually happened.

59 minutes

These days I rarely get to Oakwell except in my imagination. But in between keeping tabs on several other teams over a weekend, I watch Barnsley on iFollow. Being what are termed 'slow adopters' I see they haven't started their own TV channel yet. Much the way they haven't installed a 'big screen' at the ground. Unless you count what is possibly the smallest big screen in the upper echelons of football, which in the interests of going backwards replaced a small but bigger one they had before. It's a family club and maybe they thought someone might want to take it home when they've done with it and put it in the lounge. The stadium can look empty on TV when it isn't as the cameras capture the lower tiers whilst everyone is sitting in the higher ones or behind the operator. They need a film director never mind investment.

The last time I saw Barnsley play before this book went to press was when they were at Wembley in the 2022–23 League One Play Off Final. They were deprived of returning to the Championship by a late goal from arch rivals Sheffield Wednesday.

It's a hard life supporting them but somebody has to do it. I'll never forget the roar at Oakwell the first time I heard it echo against the tin roof of the old East Stand, now state of the art. Similarly, from the Pontefract Road (Ponty) End to which the crowd gravitated according to which way we were kicking. It's now the Norman Rimmington Stand of which more in the closing chapter.

60 minutes

On my travels I've turned out for various sides, sometimes to the surprise of team mates that I could kick a ball at all. Including as a guest for the Didcot Police XI. I think they only invited me because they thought it might give everyone a laugh, but I got my own back by scoring and refusing to be substituted unless the sergeant in charge referred it to his chief superintendent. I played for a team in Cambridge known as Mitchams Floyd FC after a local band and Michams Corner (a traffic oddity large enough to declare independence close to where Syd Barrett of Pink Floyd lived). We once played inside the highly secure Lakenheath Air Base, where the Americans treated us like royalty due to our accents, and a large crowd turned out to see airmen who normally played American Football have a go at the subtler art of soccer. I played under floodlights on an artificial pitch in Southampton for a team of lawyers and I've dabbled in parks and gardens with footballing superkids. Only the other day I saw an eight year old girl whose skills were out of this world.

I've also found myself at all manner of matches. I've followed the mixed fortunes of Burton Albion (my birth town where Branston lies), Cambridge United (when I lived opposite their Abbey Stadium as they first entered the Sunny Uplands of the football league), Bristol Rovers (why Rovers not City I don't know), Oxford United, Derby County (where I stood amongst scary supporters at the then Baseball Ground and saw their future manager Brian Clough score four goals for Middlesborough in a 7-4 victory over Derby), Winchester City (including at Birmingham City's St Andrew's Stadium when they won the FA Vase), Southampton (including as far back as Lawrie McMenemy's reign as manager: who I also met in the courtroom when he talked the bench into not disqualifying him from driving), Reading (I had a season ticket when they were in the Premier League when Cilla Black was a regular supporter and friend of then owner John Madejski), Portsmouth, Aldershot Town and Tottenham Hotspur (my son's adopted club), Farnborough Town (who I saw lose 1-5 to Arsenal in an FA Cup Fourth Round tie, making a fortune in the process) and the club Jane Austen would have been proud to play for, Hartley Wintney.

An Enjoyable Goalless Draw

Just two days before this book went to press, I see that Portsmouth played Cheltenham Town. A goalless draw may seem humdrum yet it wasn't. First an assistant referee was injured, then the fourth official who substituted for him went lame. After appeals to the crowd for anyone able to 'stand in' to save abandoning the game, a chap came forward, a Pompey supporter who Cheltenham agreed could fill the gap.

True or not, BBC Radio Gloucester implied he'd had a curry and four pints of lager before the match and had been egged on by his mates. He borrowed some gold boots and played to his fellow home supporters like a messiah before running the line to occasional applause.

Another reporter suggested games would be better if all match officials downed the chap's imagined pre-match repast and asked whether anyone at all had checked his credentials. It would be nice to think he'd never done it in his life though it seems he was a local junior league referee.

Yes, travel broadens the football mind. Amongst the bizarre things I've witnessed were Manchester United changing their kit when they were 3-0 down at half-time because they couldn't see each other on a grey day on the south coast (the game against Southampton ended 3-1), resurgent Luton Town, Bedfordshire's finest, losing to Reading at Wembley in the Simod Cup Final when we stood within a cage during the pre-Taylor Report-era (Reading won 4-1),[4] and I saw Robert Maxwell (with his now imprisoned daughter Ghislaine) presiding like royalty over games at the old Manor Ground in Oxford and nowadays find myself wondering, 'Whatever was Captain Bob thinking?' as he splashed the cash and they reached the top flight.

MY IT'S HOT TODAY. You might think climate change would make an exception for football but no it just treats the game like it does everything else. The temperature is still on the rise and they've set up a full scale drinks bar. It looks like he players will be enjoying the break and chatting as if they were in the pub for some time...

---

4. Into the Hillsborough Stadium Disaster of 1989. See https://discovery. nationalarchives.gov.uk/details/r/C9261

Tall Tale No. 5
Pundit Wars

How many football pundits does it take to change a floodlight bulb? So asked Harold Nosey-Parker of *Goal Monthly*. 'I know about the big time football commentators but there are many lesser mortals.' Football coverage and reporting is indeed fast reaching saturation point. New channels and so many hundreds of podcasts that TV commentator Sebastian Bloggs tells me he'll soon be redundant. Every fan with a shed has their own broadcasting station.

'I prefer to turn off the sound and pretend I'm at the match,' Harold Nosey-Parker said as he tried to provoke veteran commentator Syd Mumbles, President of the Shaky Soundbite Club, into an ill-considered response. Jack knew Syd always mumbled something daft if prodded. He was well-known for his eclectic nonsense, like his famous 'I think they've all flown back home' delivered from a pigeon basket on the roof of the main stand at Minster City. Mumbles it was who invented the phrase, 'It didn't went' to describe the situation where the ball travelled one way and the players the other. He also said 'Making a change was a change and I think it's made a change'.

Bored by years in the same job he would make up incidents, 'I'm sorry, we can't show you this,' he would tease viewers if the game was sluggish or the cameras fell behind the action. 'We can't show you it but somebody's on the pitch.' Sometimes if there was a break in vision, 'Betty Skyrocket, she's at it again. She's danced her way past five defenders, dribbled around the goalkeeper and slotted home on the half volley after flicking the ball over her head from behind ... but it's been disallowed.' Later when summing up he'd pretend that this imagined 'rainbow trick' was the highlight of a windswept mid-week game in which two tired teams played out a goalless draw. If the fans were chanting, 'Sign her up, sign her up, sign her up' he would turn down the background noise and say, 'They're calling for the manager to be sacked.'

A quarter of a century ago the Football You Can Trust Research Department funded a study into language used by pundits hoping that its findings might protect future generations from rogue commentators. Thirty thousand copies of the expensive report were printed, 29,987 more than needed. Those that went uncirculated were redeployed to reinforce under soil heating at various grounds around the country. Top sports archaeologist Dick Spade found a copy a few years back when Pandemonium Athletic FC knocked down parts of their old stadium in Sanatorium Avenue. Why Spade was digging around in the goalmouth in the middle of the night remains a mystery but it's been rumoured a visiting centre forward lost a gold tooth there.

The report informed readers that the two words most often used by pundits were 'football club'. A psychologist member of the research team wrote that these words created breathing space whilst the pundit thought about what to say next. Also, to connect to the masses, who immediately associated them with their own club. 'We all like to think we're at centre of the universe,' added the psychologist, 'everywhere I go I hear folk telling me why their team is the one and only one.' Next came 'training ground' as in 'a move from the training ground.' Pundits were fond of this because it suggested inside knowledge. 'However,' the report continued, 'this is pure speculation as in elite football at least these places are secured by watchtowers and guided missiles. No-one outside ever gets to see what's going on inside. Much the same way that royal commentators like to pretend they know what King Charles had for breakfast when there's an evens chance he had a piece of toast, cereals or a bit of bacon.' However 'one from the training ground' is the first complete sentence that any kid who kicks a ball is taught at nursery school.

The researchers examined lesser used but equally important snatches of commentary such as, 'He or she knows how to play football'. Blow me, that's handy. He or she's a seasoned professional who spent two years as an apprentice cleaning boots, three years at the academy and years waiting for a place in the first team. What else does he or she know about? I've seen for myself that most clubs keep a football on display in a cabinet in case any of their players forget what it is. The manager must also have reminded them what the game is all about before the match started: 'There are the goalposts, the idea is to put the ball between them. That thing hanging behind them is called a net. It's meant to catch the ball so that there can be no argument about where it went.'

The researchers concluded the same illogic applies to phrases such as, 'knows how to take a corner or throw in' and 'knows how to play without the ball.' Their report explained that this is 'why they earn vast amounts and keep a Viper SE 100K and a refurbished turbocharged Silver Whippet III in the garage.' Concerning the all embracing phrase, 'they do know how to play football' the research team decided by a majority that these words indicated that 'knowing how to play football is only half the story and far more lies behind these bare words than might appear at first glance. What they really tell us is that hard graft and intuition are no substitute for scoring more goals than the opposition.'

The Research Department suggested that spotting phrases could become a game that might add a fresh dimension to watching matches, the brainchild of two contributors. The first, John Bright, invented the idea but like a kid with a ball and no pals to play with he had to look around. That's how he and June Early came to jointly invent Pundit Wars and why on the box it says Bright and Early. But not before John and June locked themselves in a kit basket and threw words at each other.

'Second ball, calling card, hospital pass, early bath.'

'Game management, rolling back onto the pitch, running into traffic, handbags, in the locker.'

'Gift wrapped, over the moon, park the bus, getting to know each other, put up the shutters, ruffled feathers.'

'Game on, banana skin, snuck in, tough cookie, game of two halves, all across the park, front foot, half chance.'

With the aid of an abacus, they then worked out how to attach scores to these and other words which players of Pundit Wars can own during a match. The rules state that these must be picked from a hat in turn (or by using a virtual hat). Every time a word or phrase occurs, the player who owns it scores points and the one with the highest score at the end wins. Players can decide for themselves whether to carry scores forward to the next match, across the season, apply to join leagues and or knock out competitions. Whether extra time, added time and penalty shoot-outs count. Similarly, whether interviews with managers or players are included, it having been discovered that terms like 'football club', 'training ground' and 'next week' are rampant at such times, as are 'definitely (not) offside', 'definitely (not) a penalty', 'definitely (not) over the line' and 'blind as a bat'.

To give an idea of Pundit Wars in action, the rules indicate that those taking part can agree 'first to 100' or whatever number suits them. 'Players may feel more at ease with the traditional football multiples 45, 90 and 120.' For example, if 'football club' scores 2 points, 'training-ground' 5, 'he or she knows how to play football (or any other nonsensical statement)' 10, more obscure but regular ones like 'on the front foot' or 'he or she has an intelligent left foot' might score 25 and 'They think it's all over' 250.

An option for experienced players is to agree or disagree with commentators concerning VAR decisions (known as 'jokers'). The game can be played at home by two or more, remotely by teams in different time zones or hemispheres, subject to the overriding rule that everything must happen 'live' (the inventors suggesting that syndicates might otherwise benefit from transmission delays). Players can appoint a referee to argue the toss with.

What happens to pundits when they can no longer comment on games? Here it is useful to consider the experiences of four lost legends. Veteran commentator Syd Mumbles who got bored with making up things to say simply ran out of steam and opened an ice cream stall outside Vanilla Park. 'At least I get to say, "Nice one" when somebody orders a raspberry split,' he quipped. Sebastian Bloggs left the tough world of broadcasting to sell Dragon Grease door-to-door and Candy Mountain to become the first Pundit Wars ambassador at heights above 3,000 feet. Peter Dismal, the ex-goalkeeper who when his playing days ended muffed up commentating as well, was fired for being too boring. Nevertheless he went on tour giving presentations on the subject after hiring billboards saying 'Come and Enjoy a Dismal Evening'. Usually to empty houses.

Mega-rich footballers find it's a hard life playing twice a week!

Play resumes...

65 minutes

I like watching less grand sides and hoping to see a superstar in embryo. I saw Stocksbridge Park Steels' Leicester City Premier League winner and England player, Jamie Vardy in his younger days, and others like Matt Le Tissier and John Stones (of whom more in a moment).

Muscle Memory

I've also watched complete minnows. I was at one game on my local side's tree-lined village green football pitch when my mind must have wandered to my former life. As the ball came towards where I stood on the touchline I trapped it and slid it neatly to an advancing player. A sublime move. Muscle memory. One from the training ground (Oh dear even I'm saying it!). The ball hadn't crossed the line though.

The referee stared at me but wasn't sure what to do. Maybe it had never happened before. The tiny crowd looked at me quizzically as if I'd maybe invented some new rule that allowed spectator participation. After a few seconds hesitation, the referee caught up with play and carried on as if nothing had happened. The polite charm of folk who live in the backwoods!

I particularly like Aldershot Town's Recreation Ground. It has a public footpath at one end and roses behind the goal. There's something about the aroma of the turf in Jane Austen Country. It always smells sweet at Aldershot, as well as of roses at times. Modern stadia can't compete with that ... and again you couldn't make it up.

Another footballer I nudged shin pads with was Charlie Williams, whose family came from Barbados. A local lad, he defected to Doncaster Rovers before achieving TV fame as a stand-up comedian. He played 171 games for them but remarkably scored only one goal which was against his home town club Barnsley. I was at that match. He had to leave Oakwell under police escort as the crowd wanted to lynch him.

Dickie Bird, cricket umpire and former Yorkshire cricketer is another grandee from Barnsley, a supporter of its football club, who like me was rescued from the pit.[1] You couldn't make up a name like his without being told, 'Don't be silly, try again'. Like Mr Man. At our junior school we had a class teacher called just that.[2] I resisted his ire by not asking if he lived with Mrs Woman. Not a dickie bird did I say. In the Potted North 'Mrs Woman' is quite acceptable when you can't recall a woman's name. In Jane Austen Country I've heard it said that it's impolite to remember the name of someone you've only just been introduced to as it looks over familiar.

80 minutes — Cricket Break

We had a sports teacher who we named Pobble. He was awestruck by Dickie Bird. Pobble never stopped telling us that if we worked hard we too could be like the said Bird and rise above our humble stations in life. In the summer months Pobble morphed into his idol. On the field where we learnt to play a straight bat and were taught the intricacies of silly mid on using an asphalt wicket, Pobble would act as if he was presiding over a Test Match. The disused air raid shelter became the pavilion at Lords Cricket Ground and his flip chart turned into a gently unfolding scoreboard with imaginary clicks added

---

1. Bird, Michael Parkinson and (controversial) Test cricketer Geoff Boycott played with Barnsley Cricket Club. We'd see them at the ground from our school windows. On the day Boycott first played for Yorkshire I bought his ticket from him and took his place on a Civil Service day trip to Skegness (true).
2. He was actually Mr Mann with a double 'n' but that would ruin it!

by Pobble flexing his teeth. He wore a white flat cap, a white smock and he would squat, crouch, stretch, ponder and point in the precise manner of the great man before signalling 'out', 'leg before wicket', 'six' or 'no ball'. We followed his gaze, waited for his stare to flicker and watched for the tiniest of nods. Pobble not only imitated Dickie Bird, he became Dickie Bird.

So irritating did I find his posturing that one day I risked everything by screeching loudly in the manner of Edvard Munch's painting The Scream. That was me done for, I'd had my moment in the sun and feared I'd bought a one way ticket to a school for problem kids. Amazingly, Pobble didn't notice a thing, so focused was he on the task in hand, watching an imaginary Len Hutton at the crease and a pint-sized Freddie Trueman[3] about to bowl (both Yorkshiremen even if now, in Pobble's imagination, one was playing for Sri Lanka the other for Trinidad). Maybe he thought the scream was something to do with the faulty hooter of the nearby can factory. Winchester, Harrow and Eton can keep their fine pitches, our pebble strewn wicket was the only one to have hosted, on successive days, Australia, New Zealand, India and Pakistan.

Despite Pobble's plans for my future, I dreamt not of being the esteemed Bird but Harry Tufnell, scorer of the only goal in the 1912 Cup Final. This he did in true *Roy of the Rovers* fashion in the 118th minute of a replay following a 0-0 draw. Barnsley beat West Bromwich Albion 1-0.[4] Nonetheless, Pobble was adamant. We should aspire to be none other than little Dickie Birds, eventually grown up ones.

There's a statue of Dickie Bird in Barnsley where his outstretched finger has frequently proved too great a temptation for late night pranksters wanting to hang objects upon it. This despite the council raising it on a plinth.[5] There's also a statute of Barry Hines' Kes in

3. Freddie Trueman was something of a raconteur. He defined a gentleman as 'someone who got out of the bath to have a pee'.
4. If you wish to convince your friends you've done the same tell them your name's Tufnell and that it was a long time ago. Then hack their phones and such devices and remove links to Google and other search engines.
5. See *Atlas Obscura: An Explorer's Guide to the World's Hidden Wonders*. Basingstoke's 'much loved' statue of Jane Austen has avoided this fate.

the town but not one of Harry Tufnell. He like many of their long lost heros is less celebrated. Like Pongo Waring (from the 1930s) who, before he left Aston Villa (and depending on how you do the maths) was a goalscorer on a par with Erling Haaland (treble winner with Manchester City). It is said Pongo would turn up when he felt like it to train but was too good a player for this to matter. It would take another book to even scratch the surface of the aberrant geniuses of football. George Best, Paul Gascoigne, the Liverpool goalkeeper, Bruce 'Wobbly Legs' Grobbelaar, Paulo de Canio and Luis Suárez to name a few.

IT LOOKS LIKE WE ARE ABOUT TO SEE the first substitutions of the match. Both managers are going to mix things up, and quite considerably — three changes each. Except, that is, the fourth official can't find his number board. He's holding up his fingers instead, but has now realised he's not got enough digits. We could be here a while…

Tall Tale No. 6
The Trip That Changed Football

The title suggests I might be about to tell you of a really bad foul that led to football becoming less lethal. Not so, although I suppose that's near the mark as it seems women's football is much less dangerous and far more civilised. It's about a coach trip not an excruciating tackle. The story, possibly *the only true story*, of how women's football went from a game played before 20 mums and dads to filling stadiums worldwide. And about how Betty Skyrocket became a legend.

Brenda Standby was the coach driver after Alfred Redeyes called in late with the daft excuse that he had to take his dog for a walk. You can read about Brenda on the brass plaque next to the statue outside Vanilla Park that's visited by fans from every part of the known world wearing replica bus drivers' hats, holding their Vanilla 99 ice creams and waving their standby tickets.

How did it all happen? I'm glad you asked. We must go back to the day when Mr and Mrs Skyrocket, Earnest and Chick Pea, took their children Betty and her brother 'Jumping' Jack on a trip to see their first football match. A men's international. Unfortunately, there was a diversion and when they arrived at the stadium it was full. They were told that even if it wasn't they and everyone else in their party had bought dud tickets. Betty and Jumping Jack cried and jumped about like they had never done before.

'Now, now, Betty,' said Mr Skyrocket.

'Keep still Jumping Jack,' said Chick Pea cutting in. 'A quadruple whammy ... full, flannelled, frustrated and forged. How could we have been so unfortunate after putting on our best bib and tucker?'

The day had started so well even if Brenda Standby had been prickly. 'No chewing gum, no booze, no smoking, no singing, no radios, no feet on the seats and please don't put me off my driving,' she announced over the Tannoy as she headed for the motorway. 'I don't want the police arresting us all or to finish up alongside my passengers in hospital.'

There were 42 trippers, mainly those with family tickets. 'Why do we girls have to go,' grumbled Betty, 'it's a man's game, all sweat and swear words, kicking bits out of each other. Who wants to see a man's game?'

'Might learn something,' said Mr Skyrocket.

'Might not,' snapped Betty, wishing she'd stayed at home with Growler, her cat. 'I've got exams next week. I could have learnt something about triangles or manganese oxide.'

'We're about to witness The Beautiful Game and it's not often Pincushion Town has two players on opposite sides in the same international,' said Mr Skyrocket, 'Why do you think all these coaches are heading in the same direction, scarves flying from the windows.'

'Please yourself Dad, but I prefer being at home.'

The two-hour journey continued until queuing at the gate the steward shouted 'Full!'

'What d'you mean full, we've all got tickets?'

'Made on a second-rate home printer by the look of it. I'm going to confiscate those,' said the steward as a riot broke out by the entrance way to the gigantic stadium.

Sirens sounded, shields were raised, batons pointed, gas canisters prepared for action and Bert Flatbottom of Melon Ball Grocers & Son in Pincushion fell to the ground to the zap of a Taser gun fired by PC Overkill.

'That's quite enough' said Mr Skyrocket leading the rest of their party back to the coach, vowing revenge on organized crime. 'I'll get those pirates!' he exclaimed, bent on starting a campaign under the banner 'We Want Our Money Back with Interest'.

'Tell you what,' piped up Brenda Standby, 'Let's take the scenic route back, all fields and trees, get a breath of fresh air. It'll calm the nerves... a Magical Mystery Tour.' 'Mystery tour?! Magical?! What we want is a refund and compensation!'

The coach slid out of the city into leafy country lanes. Three times they turned left, then three times right. They stopped at a café where everyone got out for a cuppa or a fizzy drink, then after many lefts, rights, twists and turns, they stopped again by the roadside for several kids full of pop to be sick.

'What's all that noise across the fields?' enquired Betty.

'Here look, I've got a sat nav,' yelled an excited Jumping Jack tapping his phone. 'It's telling me that if we turn right and swing left, then follow the road on the right after the third exit on the left after the roundabout we'll come to Tinpot Town's old stadium up a track marked "You've reached your destination". The place where Tinpot men played before that sheik bought them out, gave them a new name and moved them 300 miles away to a new stadium covered in gold leaf. This here is where Tinpot Town Belles now play and there must be a match on... Let's take a peek if Brenda Standby's up for it.'

'Women playing football? Don't be daft,' Betty replied.

'Do we need tickets?' asked Chick Pea.

'Doubt it,' answered coach driver Brenda, 'if they are like some other clubs they usually open the gates after half time and it's then free.'

This is how Betty Skyrocket came to see her first women's football match and the effect was dramatic. On the journey home she was all questions. 'Why was it so exciting and how did they manage to play without the referee handing out red or yellow cards?' she asked, knowing that when they watched men's games Jumping Jack and her dad were forever shouting, 'Off, off, off!' with the commentator apologising for obscenities they might have heard. Somehow, even the grass smelled sweeter at the game she'd seen.

'How come none of the women had bandages around their heads?... Why was there no-one in the dugout with an ice pack strapped to her leg? Why were they hardly ever offside? … Do women have different brains? … Why did it look so silky smooth, whereas men flatten each other every five minutes?'

'I have to admit it's another world,' said her dad. 'It *is* football … but it's *a different game*. Even the half-time display when the parachute team of girls dropped on ropes from the roof of the stand was smartly done … That was different, too.'

For her upcoming birthday, Betty asked for her first pair of football boots. She found a club, trained hard, made it into the team and became captain. Playing for Pincushion's Vanilla Villa Vixens she won every trophy there is and led her country as well as World Women when they defeated Rest of the World's Women 5-0. The scorer of more goals than any other woman, twice as many every season than all the rest of the players in her league put together. That's why so many girls now wear Betty Skyrocket shirts and use Skyrocket Body Scrub and Toothpaste. It all began that fateful day.

Betty will never forget the day she first won the league with Vanilla Villa Vixens and they held the trophy aloft on an open top bus. Brenda Standby pulled over and joined Betty on the top deck holding the shield aloft to cheers of 'V … V … V … Vixens!'.

'A fund has been started for a statue,' reported the *Pincushion Parable*. 'It will feature Brenda, Betty and also Bert Flatbottom being Tasered'. The crowd wore special edition Vixens t-shirts and Wanda Whistlestop, Mayor of Pincushion, welcomed 'the whiff of wealthy backers wishing to invest in Vanilla Villa.' Afterwards, her assistant Catherine Wheel lit the fireworks which included 100 rockets, each signed by the entire playing squad using heat resistant ink. Their empty cases quickly became collector's items. Not only because Vixens' board of directors declared recycling one would entitle the person doing it to a half price season ticket, but also the lead set by influencer Carrie Bigweight who told her followers she'd turned hers into an artificial chrysanthemum and stuck it in a pot 'as a reminder that women's football isn't rocket science'.

Betty Skyrocket demonstrates her skills to adoring fans.

Play resumes ...

82 minutes 37 seconds

We had a genius of a sports master who it was said was a refugee. Herman the German we called him (a perfect if obvious rhyme). He frowned like a dachshund and the word was he'd been with several top clubs back home before fleeing from the Nazis. Given his contact book the Greenhoff brothers (see *page 33*) might just as easily have gone straight to Bayern Munich or Eintracht Frankfurt. Herman also taught German. What's more he chose the school football team. The classical language cohort being oversubscribed and being keen to try out something new I enrolled with four other pupils who, in the words of E L Wisty 'Never had the Latin'. By pure coincidence we comprised a centre forward, a goalkeeper, a central defender and two lads who'd chosen to play in the same position and fought it out under Herman's gaze.

Heute regnet es und diese abend keine Fußball haben wir (It's raining so there'll be no football this evening) which when cancelled was *nicht gut* (not good). I soon found that the German language sometimes involves thinking back to front. To make matters worse there are no words for some things we take for granted, which means going round the houses as if you're explaining them to a young child. But it's a fascinating way of keeping the brain active.

Another local teacher who made a mid-life career change is the late Brian Glover, whose playground game between an imaginary Manchester United and Tottenham Hotspur in the film of Barry Hine's novel *Kes* is an all time classic. Glover became Manchester United's No. 9, living the part, as he did in roles at the National Theatre, where he even played God. A secondary school teacher he moonlighted as the no holds barred wrestler Leon Arras the Man From Paris in the days of Giant Haystacks and Jackie Pallo. If Barry Hines, Barnsley born author of *Kes* is allowed to imagine such things, including the way Glover's character upstages his smirking pupils, so can I. Hines played football for Barnsley Reserves, had a trial for Manchester United and represented England Grammar Schools. Like myself, Dickie Bird and others he belongs to the ranks of those rescued from a life in the mines by a random twist of fate. To acquaint yourself with a passable Barnsley stereotype, do study Brian Glover[1] in the scene I've mentioned.[2]

85 minutes

There have been many outstanding players at Oakwell over the years, the best-known of which must be Tommy Taylor who Barnsley sold to Manchester United for a then record transfer fee of £29,999 (a pound off to avoid big headedness). Tragically, Taylor, who also played for England, was one of the victims of the Munich air crash. He was laid to rest in Barnsley.

When I was growing up I remember Arthur Kaye, a right winger who would run four or five defenders ragged. He might be compared to Jack Grealish of Manchester City and England, or Lioness Lauren James. Kaye knew how to pull defenders into committing a foul, especially in the penalty box. The home fans knew it as soon as he received the ball—the place literally trembled. Kaye was sold to Blackpool[3] for £20,000 as a replacement for the all time great of English football, Stanley Matthews, and later went to Middlesborough and Colchester United. He never played for England but should have. Kaye did make the Under-23 squad and the preliminary cohort from which an England World Cup 22 was chosen.

---

1. Yet another alumni of Barnsley Grammar School.
2. https://www.whosampled.com/movie/Kes/Manchester-United-vs-Spurs/
3. Blackpool also play in Outcast Orange: see my Tall Tale about Old Soss.

Kaye's team mate on the left flank was an equally unplayable and elusive Scotland B international, Johnny McCann whose hair was plastered down with so much Brylcream that the ball slid off his head. Down the middle was a lolloping, high scoring, No. 9, Lol Chappell with a record six hat-tricks for Barnsley. In my Tale Tales within this book his feat would have been upgraded to 'all in the same game after coming on as a substitute in the 74th minute.'

Standing Room Only

Among other Oakwell players of the time was Bert Tindill, who hit the bar with a superb, long range shot in the sixth round of the FA Cup at Leicester City's old Filbert Street stadium to leave the score 0-0. Barnsley lost the replay at Oakwell. It was an afternoon game (floodlights came late to a town that had only just stopped using gaslight) and, after a lot of argy bargy, the schools were closed to avoid what the newspapers described as a strike by pupils.

I still meet people who say, 'I was there'. I believe the attendance stands as a post-war record, just under 40,000, standing mostly.

I once sold a washing machine to Bert Tindill doing a summer job. He came into the shop because I knew his niece. People in the Potted North were funny like that. I think that today Bert would have ordered it by smartphone after comparing the meerkat.

The high flying football managers Neil Warnock (over 15 different clubs), Mick McCarthy (Republic of Ireland and several leading clubs) and Paul Heckingbottom all played for Barnsley, the last of these having also managed the club and recently steered Sheffield United back into the Premier League. I saw an interview session in which Warnock and McCarthy appeared side by side as managers of competing clubs. Warnock said that McCarthy used to clean his boots. As I've said, you need to know how to handle banter in football. McCarthy just smiled as many folk in the Potted North do. I'm reminded of a similar put down. If someone was acting marginally above their station in those parts, the stock response was along the lines, 'Her mother used to do our washing but we sacked her for eating soap'.[4]

I SEE THERE'S A CHAP IN A SUIT on the touchline waving a scrap of paper. Those rumours about state of the club's finances might just be true. I think someone's trying to rustle up enough hard cash to pay the electricity bill and in the meantime the guy's going to disconnect the floodlights and seize three of our players. In the meantime it's every fan to their phones to help lighten the darkness…

4.   If you wanted to really make a point it would be 'piddling on the doorstep'.

Tall Tale No. 7

Strange Games

There are many types of football. Forgettable games too when players don't try at all or belligerent ones when they're on go slow over unpaid wages. 'You can lead a footballer to the pitch but you can't make him or her kick the ball' football historian Spud Wisdom wrote in his book *My Parents Grew Me From Seed*. He described the times when he and his sister Sprout were taken in a colander to stone circles where their mum and dad would use ancient monuments for goalposts. 'All part of the rich tapestry of an alternative lifestyle' he wrote.

Soccer seamstress Gongs Galore has created a rich tapestry of her own. A 30 metre wall-hanging entitled 'We Woz Robbed' it depicts the history of football mostly using match stick figures embellished with balls, scarves, hooters and tubs of Dragon Grease. This chapter is based on a preview of this wall-hanging but ignores Spud's work entirely.

There have been games with huge scorelines and those with no score at all but as far as I know no minus results. They range from Vanilla Villa Vixens' 23-0 victory over Tinpot Town Belles to the day Concrete Castle set up a flat back ten in their game with Park the Bus United. From games in which so many players received a red card that the referee collapsed exhausted, to those in which a disputed winning goal was scored in the 99th minute or a penalty kick entered the net after the ball first hit both goalposts and the crossbar three times. Things talked about for years in pubs, clubs and, in the case of gasping referees, resuscitation units.

Gongs Galore's tapestry depicts a number of strange games in a section marked 'Altogether Different'. It shows everything from football whilst paragliding from a cliff edge to playing the game in a hot tub. There is even a colony of cubists who tried playing with square balls. This caught on with free-thinkers until the authorities asked Professor Naomi Fitz-Nicely of Long Forgotten University to look into things. She concluded far too much time was being spent standing on the ball and posing for selfies before it was decided by the football authorities that round balls were to be preferred. By a majority of 29 to 1.

As shown in We Woz Robbed, walking football is for those who prefer a slower way of life than exists in most sports or are old enough to remember taking part in the Battle of Vapour Rub. It's meant to be played at pedestrian pace not at a sprint or wearing hiking boots. It has reached a level of sophistication, with trophies and a pension club. Problems have arisen from cheating, playing faster than the rules allow or teams fielding Olympic athletes in disguise. Knee-ball the tapestry shows is a game best played during a picnic. It was devised by Cecil Sandwich who when offered a cup of tea and a bun as he was about to play the ball said, 'Thank you kindly, I really *kneeded* that'.

One Kick, as picked out in gold thread by Gongs Galore, is played by people living close to walls, especially those without windows. The tapestry shows an estate agent telling players that dwellings which enjoy the constant thud of ball against brick are slow to sell. The One Kick Gable End Trophy attracts players from many nations. The rules are simple: each player is allowed a single kick of the ball with which to land it against the wall. The idea is to make it bounce far away so that it is hard for the next player, preferably in a prickly bush. It can be played by any number or even alone by those who gain satisfaction from beating themselves.

Contrary to popular belief Table Football isn't a game in which players mount the kitchen table. The tapestry shows tiny players made out of plastic, wood, tin or marzipan. These are set out on a cloth made to resemble a football pitch. In other versions players are encased in a cabinet and attached to each other by rods so that they can swivel and perform somersaults. Model players should be distinguished from role models and also from those players who parade about in advertisements wearing designer clothes.

I'm afraid that space prevents me from describing all the different versions of football that exist including the many e-games but as Gongs Galore has identified and you will be able to see if ever her work comes on tour to your neck of the woods they include those cross-bred with tennis, netball, hockey and cooking as seen in the popular TV programme Masterkick. It will be going on show so please keep an eye out for announcements.

I do however need to mention one version of the game for its sheer audacity. The distinctive features of Oval Ball are that it is played using H-shaped goalposts, an elongated ball and hands as well as feet. It involves bodily interferences, missing teeth, flat noses and gruesome stares. It is not unknown for players to devour each other. Even its less psychotic participants frequently employ what is known as a flying tickle (or perhaps I misheard and that should be flying tackle). The ball resembles a prune inflated to 100 times its natural size.

Oval ball comes in two varieties, 'Oval Leek' and 'Oval Onion'. Historically, oval onion was played by rank amateurs (including ladies, gentlemen and posh folk) and oval leek by professionals (bounty hunters, mercenaries and those on the run). In the early days organizers experimented (as the soccer authorities did) with a square ball. It was a chap called Dice who asked 'Do I kick it or chuck it to see which side lands face up?' and his friend Ben Tossit who replied 'Give it a try!' After a hiatus during which an oblong ball was used for three seasons all that remained was to figure out how to score. It was agreed that travelling with the ball over the opponents' goal line whilst grinding the teeth as it hit the ground best fitted the word 'try'. Tossit also shouted 'Five' as he counted the bumps on his forehead so that the score was settled there and then.

The tapestry shows games played by 15 or 13 a side except when there are nine, seven, five or less. It depicts players as a maniacal lot who as soon as look at you will kick you to the Frozen Stiff Islands if they think it means winning. Top leek players are shown carrying away small fortunes by handcart. However modern day oval onion players are also shown being awarded vast sums to confound the issue. It captures line ups (which experts have pointed out some people mistakenly call 'line outs') that resemble a guard of honour turning into a mid-air game of pass the parcel after the ball has been lofted skywards from the touchline. Unlike with proper football, where a key aim is to keep the ball on the pitch, the tapestry shows oval ball players kicking it way out of the stadium to a place called 'Tudge'.

We Woz Robbed contains three versions of the origins of oval ball. First, Dame Penny Whistle, head of Privet Hedge Academy, being called to a chemistry lab as an experiment went wrong. This blew out the doors and windows and caused everyone to grab each other by the waist and push in different directions. 'Scrum' she yelled for some unexplained reason. Next, Bavarian bin scavengers playing the aristocratic party game *Überball,* the forerunner of oval onion and the peasant pastime *Unterball,* the progenitor of oval leek. This at a time when they also experimented by combining the game with an oompah band and festive dancing. Finally, and less convincingly the fake news that both games can be traced to the Pharaohs and that The Sphinx is crouching over the first oval ball.

Gongs Galore is also careful not to miss the tale of Benny Awayday who missed the oval ball lesson when his chums learned the rules. He was stuck up a tree collecting nuts. In the days before the internet poor Benny never recovered from this gap in his knowledge. He didn't understand what the game was all about and was too proud to ask. When he first tried the library the *Secret Book of Oval Ball* was out on loan, the next time it was on a high shelf marked 'Restricted Reading'. On the sole occasion Benny was selected to play oval ball (due to being mistaken for his lookalike, superstar Brendan Skullcap) he dribbled and headed the ball as if he was a soccer ace on a mission.

At first everyone thought they were seeing things but as he kicked the ball between the H-shaped posts crying, 'Goal … What's happened to the net?' Benny was removed from the pitch with a boat hook. He was given a red card and never played the game again.

Like Benny, most soccer fans prefer not to think about oval ball. It keeps them awake at night. Oval Ball Nightmares is a certifiable condition as it can induce severe and unpleasant reactions in those who have not inherited the correct gene.

Back to the future, or at least the present, and football can be played on a phone, a computer or in virtual reality. I'm told lazy gamers can set the controls so football teams play by themselves and return to watch a replay. Those involved can buy clubs, managers or players using crypto-currency. Cases have been reported of children bank-rupting their parents who thought they were buying real life players not digital ones. I have a friend who suffered this fate so please let me know if you would like to buy a second hand Mo Salah or well used Lionel Messi.

I must now shoot to the local park where we're playing a game involving all my favourite rules: no offside, a ten goal start, score and you're in goal and only kick with your weaker foot. It ends when it gets dark. If you'd like to watch it will be on catch up. It's being captured on the park's CCTV in a format allowing you to swap the images of you and your friends for ours.

Bavaria experimented with an oblong ball, music and dancing.

Play resumes...

90 minutes

I'll allow myself one more pick from the players who, like Dennis Law did at Huddersfield Town, kept Barnsley from lowering their sights in my direction. Duncan Sharpe really was 'whistled up from the pit'. He played over 200 games for the club before joining Bedford Town. One of a succession of armour-plated centre halves, I was there the day he had his teeth loosened. A heavily built player but as agile as he was solid, he was frequently seen spitting blood. There are not many jobs where everything depends on your last performance and you have to chew the carpet to ease the pain.

One of Oakwell's best-known graduates of modern times is John Stones from Penistone, who left Barnsley for Everton then moved to Manchester City where he was one of their treble winning team of 2022–2023. He's a mainstay of the England team. I must give him a 'Triple Whammy Award' for players who've shared the air of St George's Park, Oakwell and the local moors.

Just Like Watching Hartley Wintney...

Penistone Church FC. There's a name for a made up team if it wasn't taken. Though to my mind it would consist of vicars, bell ringers rising on ropes to head the ball and players on loan from The Saints at Southampton FC. An organist would play and the fans would sing 'It's just like watching Hartley Wintney' and there'd be stained glass in the changing room windows. A snack bar with grouse sandwiches. Plates by the turnstiles labelled 'Collection'.

I'm sure you'll be able to add tales of your own. Should you wake up thinking 'These flashbacks are driving me nuts, I wonder if I can get something for it from the chemist?' write it down before it disappears. Cheer yourself up by pretending you've just won a medal playing The Beautiful Game. Make friends with the delivery driver who's killing time waiting for offers play in the a multi-trillion riyal Saudi Pro League.

Why not call yourself Lord Whoever or Dame Whatsit. I didn't use the real 'gongs' earned by people I've mentioned in the text in case you thought I was making them up. They appear in the Index. I bumped into a well-known football manager recently. He said that when he collected his MBE the taxi driver took him to the back door of the palace. 'Aren't we going in the front,' he asked. The driver replied, 'No, this is where I went in when I got mine.' Don't forget this when you get yours. Send me your details and I'll mention it to Charles and Camilla if ever they drop in for a game of Pundit Wars.

OH DEAR ME THERE'S A PROTEST against the club's owners who are apparently planning to move the stadium to Timbuktu and build blocks of flats here. It's getting out of hand and the ref's taken the players off until it cools down. They've chained themselves to the goalposts. Does anyone have a pair of bolt cutters...?

Tall Tale No. 8

Dragon Grease

A nyone who knows anything about football knows about Dragon Grease. This heavily marketed potion, the formula for which is a well-guarded secret, can be found in dressing-rooms, kitchens, bedrooms, bathrooms, tool sheds and kit bags the world over.

'I keep a tub on the mantelpiece and 20 in the cupboard,' runs the enticing TV advertisement whilst the jingle from the star-spangled chorus line reminds viewers, 'The only thing we know is that every-where we go, Dragon Grease always steals the show'. It's said that for every penny spent on anything around the entire world 80 per cent goes on this magical substance. In part due to its many uses and mysterious qualities. The makers sponsor football clubs, players' shirts and football goings on galore, mostly courtesy of Naming Rights Incorporated and their sister company Unfortunate Tattoos.

Dragon Grease only arrived in this country in modern times after Ali Sage-Whittington, a descendant of its inventor, arrived here bearing a tub in concentrated form on the sailing ship *Quirk of Fate*. Legend has it that the formula was stitched safely inside his undergarments. The records show that Dragon Grease was created by his ancestor, a mystic known as The Sage who lived in a cave on a Far Continent.

'I dwell in the cave for peace of mind,' the mystic remarked, 'I can't stand the pace of life so I kip out here where I can communicate with the Cosmos ... I'm called The Sage.'

The Sage became so disoriented by his sagacious ways that he scribbled down things he might not recall when his faculties returned to Earth. He wrote 'starfish', 'jelly', 'cardamom', 'camphor', 'carrot juice', 'stir', 'don't shake' and 'bake for a week and a half' all of which came to him at different times. He decided to try out what he'd written down by stirring the ingredients together, being careful not to shake them. As time went by he took to producing the mixture in vats and labelling them 'Family Secret'.

The Sage first tried consuming the mixture for lunch. Due to its bitterness he next tried adding chilli powder, finally a whole bag of chillies, which scorched his delicate Sage-type innards. 'Never again,' he groaned as he was stretchered away, 'Time for Plan B.' Plan B was to add black ink and sell the mixture as boot polish. It was at this point fate again took one of its pre-booked twists and turns. Just as his assistant's helper's errand runner, Jara Jam, was about to dip her sandals in a vat of Family Secret she noticed the water had evaporated leaving the remaining ingredients intact. She fell over in surprise before discovering that what remained was good for relieving the bumps and bruises she suffered in the process.

'Eureka,' shouted Jara Jam, 'The Sage had the answer all along, why ever did he bother to add the ink, the transcendental muppet?' The answer remains one of The Seven Mysteries of Parsley, Sage and Time. Errand runner Jara Jam immediately sped to the cave of The Sage crying, 'I think we have something here ... you must have lost the plot!'

'We?' said The Sage. 'Well, I mean "you" have something here ... And maybe "we" just a little bit,' Jara replied. 'Not just something,' The Sage continued, 'I think we've found the Holy Grail ... Not the missing one, but the one that will change the world. Especially the world of football!'

'Football?'

'Yes, football,' answered The Sage, 'I have absolutely no idea what it is, but I saw the word in a cloud ... I think it must be some kind of game and in my stream of unconsciousness the players were rubbing the mixture all over themselves.'

'What's the stuff called?' asked Jara.

'Family Secret' answered The Sage. 'That's what I've put on the labels, Family Secret so I'm not telling you.'

'You can't call it that,' said the marketing-minded Jara, 'it sounds too up itself. What did those in the dream call it?'

'I woke up before I could ask,' answered The Sage, 'but I think they said Damp Jelly Stuff.'

'Don't you have to keep it cool and under ground?' queried Jara, 'Why not Dungeon Juice? ... Maybe Dam Jam ... It's certainly thick enough to hold back the Great Tidal River of Gooseberry Fish at the bottom of the garden?'

'I'm not having that,' said The Sage, 'you're just trying to get your name in on the act and that might well confuse people about who owns the recipe ... and those who don't read the instructions might spread it on toast. I think we should call it Doom Oil, or Dripping Oil, or maybe even Donkey Dung?'

'Eureka ... Dragon Grease!' yelled Jara.

'Whatever,' replied The Sage, who was losing interest in earthly matters and drifting into another temporary release from the planet. So, Dragon Grease it was. All that was needed was for football to be invented.

Many years later, after The Sage communed with the stars one final time and went to join them, the formula passed to his seventh wife, Even Sager, and then down the family line under ancient law through a myriad of Sages, girls, boys and other human forms until it landed firmly in the lap of the entrepreneurial Ali Sage-Whittington. Ali, it was, who set off on the *Quirk of Fate* to seek his fortune, having heard that the streets of a small island somewhere in a cooler clime were covered in paving slabs. He'd also heard the roads were fitted with cat's eyes so he rounded up Ginger his cat, packed his bags, rang for the chauffeur and jumped into the back of his Horseless Carriage SX 1000. 'I would have travelled by air,' he informed baffled friends, 'but Ginger doesn't like flying ... and Dragon Grease weighs a ton in condensed form.'

Sage-Whittington went first to Minster then to Pincushion, next to Tinpot and finally to Middle Place, the centre of the stir it and see industry. There he set up a factory producing huge quantities of Dragon Grease until he had so much that he was forced to acquire a bottomless sump, Stinker's Lagoon, into which millions of new batches were laboriously ladled by egg spoon. By spoon after spoon the lagoon filled and filled. But owning a vast subterranean Dragon Grease lake didn't automatically mean selling shed loads of the substance. Not until Ali stumbled across an unusually sharp-witted guy called Dick Smart, manager of Middle Place Wanderers.

'Tell you what,' Smart told Ali after entertaining him to a meal in the fourth gourmet restaurant on the left in Middle Place High Street, 'Give me a tub of Dragon Grease every week for the lads and some publicity stickers and I guarantee you that I'll empty Stinker's Lagoon faster than you can say "Unblock my U-bend".' 'Done,' agreed Ali, desperate not to miss the one offer he couldn't refuse if Dragon Grease was ever to see the light of day. The modern history of the product and its use around the world owes much to that seismic moment.

Football is just one of the professions where the product is now used to protect the skin, make it shine and repair it whether broken or not. It is not just a soothing substance that makes you glow like radioactivity. Neither is it just for cramp and the perils of running around on lush turf. The *Guess What's Happened Book of Records* states that it is 'The most used, fastest acting and universally adored resident of medicine cupboards, beauty parlours and back street garages the world over.' Dragon Grease can be used for polishing brass knockers, trapping squirrels, mending pots and pans, stopping fleeing motorists, walking upside down on the ceiling, blocking out loud music (when spooned into the ear) and lighting fires. It has been tested by experts in white coats who have awarded it a High as a Kite Mark and found it indestructible. They declared that 'Even if the world were to end tomorrow at least there might still be a huge cloud of Dragon Grease in the atmosphere above where Stinker's Lagoon used to be. It overcame the great starfish famine of last February so why not Armageddon?'

Ali Sage-Whittington, grandson six times over of The Sage, is well-respected in the community. He has become a philanthropist who also collects copious numbers of copyrights and patents. He and his cat Ginger have become welcome guests at all manner of events but are so wealthy from sales of Dragon Grease that neither needs to be present in person when having their nails clipped. Dragon Grease has indeed become a global brand, some say the brand of all brands. The Dragon Grease logo appears on handbags, football shirts and billboards. The potion is endorsed by A-list celebrities whilst B-listers and influencers pay thousands to be seen rubbing it on themselves.

The cave where The Sage once lived now bears a plaque in 27 languages recording that long lost Eureka moment. Jara Jam's descendants still receive a royalty of half a per cent and Middle Place Wanderers have installed a life size replica of The Cave of The Sage outside their football ground, with its onion-shaped retractable roof, now renamed The Sage and Onion Stadium. Dick Smart is the well-oiled President of Middle Place Wanderers and the club still receive a free tub of Dragon Grease every week, with a bonus tub if anyone scores a hat-trick.

Play resumes…

Stoppage time

Where did the stories in this book come from? Tall Tale No. 1 about Stanley Accrington is (quite obviously) based on Accrington Stanley, a club made famous by a Milk Marketing Board advertisement in which a lad asks, 'Accrington Stanley… Who are they?' This at a time when the name had all but vanished after the original club, which reached old Division Four of the English Football League then played in the Lancashire Combination, folded. At the end of 2005–2006, their modern-day incarnation gained entry to the Football League (EFL) where they've played as high as today's League One. My story about 'Akkers' stems from my earliest contact with football when I stood watching a classmate in goal. Why had he been secretly picked? I was the one who *distracted* Ronnie Cloggs. The reason he let in the only goal of the game was all my fault. I'd sensed something wasn't right and struck a blow for the rest of my classmates in the hope he wouldn't be allowed to jump the queue again.

I didn't break the window of Ray Haddocks Fish & Chips with a header in order to be 'spotted' by a talent scout but we did have such an establishment. Covered in rosettes it was. We placed our regular order ending '…and a few bits for the dog'. They were the tastiest part of the meal and maybe the dog got a look in here and there.

What happened is that we were practicing by the local College of Art using its ornamental gateposts for goalposts. My searing header smashed one of the matching lanterns atop the columns. No big deal ordinarily. Being honest kids and the police station close by we reported the incident. We were given the third degree and kept for as long as they dared in a windowless room as we protested our innocence. It maybe tinged my view of confessions, true or false. As a lawyer I now know we should have said 'No comment' however suspicious this sounds. Months later an envelope dropped through the letter box containing a demand for a large sum. Both lanterns needed replacing so they'd match. It turned out they were a poor man's Lalique-type set. They may have been affordable when the college installed them but the price had rocketed. The fear of my parents that they were heading for Debtors Yard meant they settled the arm and a leg bill immediately. I repaid them week by week from the proceeds of my newspaper round.

Celebrity News Round

My greatest claim to fame is that I delivered Arthur Scargill's newspapers.[1] I handed him his *Daily Worker* (the only copy west of Vladivostok) at Camelot, his union's castellated mansion. It was a chap from there who set up Pogmoor Panthers' game against the USSR.

Next I dropped off *The Times* to dapper Roy Mason MP often seen at Oakwell puffing his pipe. He was Secretary of State for Northern Ireland and a friend of his equally pipe dependent boss Prime Minister Harold Wilson, a Huddersfield Town supporter. I hesitated but decided not to ask the pair to intervene concerning my non-selection by Wilson's team. Lord Mason (as he became) was the only person to have his delivery boy searched by an armed guard at a sentry box. I decided not to try slipping in a show reel.

More importantly, I delivered the *Sporting Life* to Johnny Steele who managed Barnsley FC and took them to the Sixth Round of the FA Cup. Like our sports master Herman the German he had a scrunched up face and puffed away as if his life depended on it, so I assumed all football coaches did that. I'd wear my replica football shirt and kick a tin can along the gutter hoping he'd glance up from sticking a pin in the horses.

---

1. For younger readers, Arthur led the miners' strike that contributed to the toppling of Prime Minister Ted Heath's Government. When he tried the same with Margaret Thatcher she used the term 'the enemy within'. I've often wondered who she meant.

Superfan Hyam Keenbritches (Tall Tale No. 2) is an amalgam of supporters who know everything there is to know about football and more. Football is a subject where everyday supporters absorb news of scores, transfers, takeovers and gossip by osmosis and without apparent effort. A phenomenon I've heard those not interested in football marvel at. More and more football-related information enters the Cosmos but fans still manage to keep up with it. Hyam is a metaphor for all die hard supporters, his jetpack a motif for the way football's changing. From VAR to drones to goal-line technology to statistics and 20 or more matches a day on TV or online to chose from. Starting at breakfast time with Yokohama Jets and ending at bedtime with Philadelphia Union. In between times English, French and Italian games, the Saudi Pro League and re-runs of old matches. Hyam knows each and every result, player, ranking and blade of grass since the dawn of time.[2]

I knew a guy who as youngsters we called Old Soss. I used his catchy nickname in the story of The Outcasts in Tall Tale No. 3. The individual who built Paradise Park is an amalgam of do it yourself types who are on a mission. Dan Treacle (Old Soss) is their flag bearer, self-appointed, hands-on, building a Theatre of Dreams out of thin air. One chap I knew really did fence off common land. He put up a stand and surrounded the pitch with corrugated iron crowd barriers taken from the sheds people had there (some may still have been in use). He cut the half-time oranges, planted the corner flags and washed the team's kit. There were others like him who found their way into the story of the Pig's Ear of a stadium that became Paradise Park.

The Goalkeepers' Convention (Tall Tale No. 4) reprises my outings on the conference trail whilst transposing this to an unlikely group of delegates. I have a photograph of real life goalkeeper Harry Hough an the platform at a tamer event when a strike by footballers was being planned. He looks as eager as Owen Gole was towards his seminar group. Letting things get out of hand was a nod to the fact that conference goers arrive hesitant, tell everyone how much better

---

2.   Lawyers say 'time immemorial' which dates from 1189. Heaven knows why!

they do things back home, but by the last evening most are the best of friends even though they might hardly meet each other again. I just turned the rumbustious farewell into a riot.

'They're All Bloomin' Criminals'

I've met real life academics like Professor Fitz-Nicely who can construct devilish theories at such events. In my imagination I applied to her prestigious Long Forgotten University to complete a thesis of my own called 'Crime and Football: Is It the Freshly Cut Grass?'

I'd mapped out squads from several countries each of which could field an entire team of real life players who'd served time in prison. An impressive list that included big names and every crime in the criminal calendar.[3]

The world-class referee who told me 'They're all blooming criminals' does exist. It happened at an event in Newcastle, home to resurgent Newcastle United. I'd just named my Criminal Justice XI of English players who'd hit the skids. In truth, football's no more likely to produce black sheep than other professions. I could do the same with lawyers, politicians, bankers, musicians, business moguls and vicars.

I have a virtual notepad to collect words and phrases during matches and the game of Pundit Wars (Tall Tale No. 5) flows from hearing repetitive or banal remarks. You can play a similar but different game by selecting a letter and spotting words beginning with say P, Q or Z that occur in a commentary. Choose your own letters. If you're a Liverpool supporter you may prefer L. Ws and vowels if you follow Wolverhampton, Wycombe, Wigan or Wimbledon, R if your team's Blackburn Rovers. Maybe S if you follow Sunderland, Swindon Town or Splott Albion.[4]

---

3. The right to be forgotten prevents me naming them here.
4. Splott Albion FC play in the Cardiff and District Premier League.

Oops there goes another...

As England Women beat Nigeria Women in the first knock out round of the 2022–23 Women's World Cup, I heard a new candidate. The commentator said that the referee had made a 'decisive decision'. Quite decisive. To award England a penalty. The decisiveness of her decisive decision was not however her final decision, decisive or otherwise.

The more the clock ticked the more it became clear that her decisive decision might have to be undecided which it was by her next even more decisive decision following her decision to go to the pitch side monitor and review the decisive decision she'd first made this time using VAR.

I'm taking a sabbatical from collecting more 'bloopers' as I've started to feel like superfan Hyam Keenbritches must when storing endless facts and figures. I'm no longer that keen.

The Trip That Changed Football (Tall Tale No. 6) merges memorable outings by coach with the rise of women's football. Betty Skyrocket was inspired by Hannah McTavish my Pogmoor Panthers teammate. No-one ever asked questions about the girl who played on our left flank or seemed to think this at all odd. What a trailblazer. Just like Betty.

Concerning 'the whiff of investors' in Betty's team (or the town of Pincushion) I still chuckle that one club close to where I live now was kept alive when the bank held off for a few days due to an entirely false bid from a crackpot. A guy well-known as 'The Doyen of Daft Ideas'. Nonetheless he kept his finger in the dyke long enough for a real backer to emerge and the only reason the club didn't fold was his madcap involvement. It's difficult to separate him from big-time chancers bidding to take over top clubs, strip their assets and build flats where their ground once stood. Some not knowing where the money will come from and fast footing it to raise the cash. Funny takeovers have happened to several real life clubs despite porous 'fit and proper person' rules. Tinpot Town suffered a similar fate and it remains to be seen whether the gold leaf on their new stadium peels off in the rain.

My less than believable chapter about Strange Games (Tall Tale No. 7) includes threads from life. *Überball* and *Ünterball* reprise my fascination with the German language and how German sentences work. Not really back to front as I said earlier but in a different way to English ones. I've heard that German and broad Yorkshire (the strongest of Yorkshire dialects) are not so far apart.[5] I certainly took to the language like a duck to Tinker's Pond (on which Stinker's Lagoon is based) that lies by the village of Wilthorpe, where I lived as a young child and later washed windows for half a day, before walking off the job and returning to the Town Hall to see Ms Pinkerton about why she hadn't found me a job in football. There is a legend that Tinker's Pond has no bottom. How that works I don't know but I've heard talk of mineshafts, tunnels and the odd cyclone of saltwater. Just the place to store Dragon Grease though (Tall Tale No. 8).

The Unseen Impact of a Red Card

I was the pupil who missed the school lesson about the rules of Rugby. Laid up in hospital having my tonsils removed, not stuck up tree collecting nuts (or in an earlier draft suffering from Pancake Disease a harmless once a year health hazard). I never caught up and I really did get sent off for treating the game like one of soccer. Everyone looked bemused as I dribbled with the ball, trapped it neatly underfoot, flicked it in the air and headed it towards what to me seemed rather unusual H-shaped goalposts. It's hard to do this when the ball isn't round but I managed it. Our captain that day, Dave Rollitt, went on to play for Barbarians, Wakefield, Bristol and England. That's just how thin the line is between greatness and ignominy. He put his arms around my shoulders as perplexed as anyone and asked, 'Are you okay?'

---

5. Yorkshire's Anglo-German language connection is I believe to do with foreign marauders chatting to locals sitting around a well under an oak tree.

In a soccer era of endless back passes, physical goings on, shirt pulling and looping 25 yard throw ins the difference between soccer and rugby is less marked than it was. Herman the German taught us soccer using his back to front instructions so I should have known all about passing the ball to the player behind me. He was also the housemaster I had to account to for the mortal sin of being sent off. My ambitions to play any kind of game might have been greater had I not blotted my copy book. Gary Lineker never got sent off and neither did I apart from that day. My modern day oval ball experiences are limited to traffic jams caused by those attending international matches at Twickenham, which served to reinforce the jitters I got for years each time rugby was mentioned. *Chacun à son goût* (each to their own preference) as the badge I've designed for French side Catalan Dragons says.

Tall Tale No. 8, Dragon Grease, is inspired by Dog Oil, a real life ointment that smells ever so slightly of petroleum jelly. But I've altered the ingredients to be climate friendly. The story has no further connection to Dog Oil except that I keep a tub of the real stuff handy. The tale is a mix of the myths and legends that grow up around the tiniest things thing and are often milked, as Dragon Grease was, until the udders are sore. The imagined advertising jingle is my version of a punch line in a song by writer, singer and satirist Leon Rosselson that takes pot shots at another global product: 'The only thing I know is that everywhere I go the Coca Cola always tastes the same'.

Tall Tale No. 9, The Cup Final, which comes in a few pages time, is based around the notion that every footballer worth his or her Epsom Salts wants to play in such a game and if lucky score the winning goal. The tale builds on an episode in the life of yours truly at Hull City which underpins it. That's because Cliff Britton, the manager there, really did call me into his office in the way Teddy Toughnut did Peter Pikelet[6] and ask, 'What would you do if you weren't to play football?'. My reply was less ambitious than Peter's 'I think I'll be Prime Minister.'[7]

---

6. Pikelet is what folk in the Potted North who prefer Ps call a crumpet.
7. George Weah became President of Liberia. He played with some of the best clubs internationally and in the UK with Manchester City and Chelsea (where he won the FA Cup). He was also FIFA World Player of the Year in 1995.

'A lawyer,' I said. I don't know why other than bravado. I'd no idea what a lawyer was but it sounded grand (and turned out to be prophetic).[8]

The Mona Lisa of the Potted North

Laughing is one thing, smiling is its poor relation. However there's an old saying that a smile is worth 1,000 footballs. Smiling is something that comes naturally to folk in the Potted North. If you do that where I live now you risk them dialing 999. I first noticed this in Cambridge where heads point downwards. According to poet Rupert Brooke, Cambridge people 'rarely smile, being urban, squat, and packed with guile'.[9] Turning this on its head, Potted North folk 'always smile, if you don't they run a mile'. Except if you do it on the football pitch they think you've gone soft.[10] I've seen referees flash their teeth to diffuse bad situations. Sometimes a false smile like a used car salesman. You can add this to things to spot. One of Art History's lesser-known facts is that the Mona Lisa was inspired by a chance encounter between Leonardo da Vinci and one of the office girls at Barnsley FC who gave him an enigmatic smile when she brought him his cuppa. He was chosen over Canaletto to re-design the East Stand. Canaletto was the jobbing artist who painted the Dearne and Dove Canal after mistaking Worsborough Bridge for the Bridge of Sighs.

BLOW ME AWAY THERE'S A FLARE ON THE PITCH and its burned a huge hole in the six yard box. They've put out a call for six tipper trucks of topsoil and 20 bags of sand...

---

8.   Another strange law-based but true phantom is from the days when we learned to take penalties with Sandy Soot. My friends came up with the nickname 'Barrister' for me which they later shortened to 'Barry'. If you repeat any word over and over it can begin to sound hilarious. They did this falling about laughing. Serendipity.

9.   'The Old Vicarage, Grantchester'.

10. I've included instructions for looking fierce earlier in the book.

Tall Tale No. 9
Cup Finals

I t is fitting that a chapter about Cup Finals should appear at the end of this collection of short stories. The most exciting games can come at the end of a long hard season it's true, but cup finals are sometimes tense and trying affairs for supporters. I'll try and liven things up. Football teams like to win a trophy and every player worth their salt wants to score the winning goal in the most prestigious game of all so they can tell their great grandkids' grandkids about it.

As young football hopeful Peter Pikelet told hard bitten Teddy Toughnut, manager of Tinpot Town, at the end of Pikelet's first term studying the Lost Art of Football at Tinpot Town Academy when pressed as to his ambitions, 'I want to score the winning goal in the Cup Final'.

'Don't they all,' said Toughnut hiding his incredulity. 'We like players on a mission … You must be the chap they've told me about who learned to run before he came off the feeding bottle … But tell me … What would you do if you weren't to play football for a living?'

'Oh,' said young Pikelet thinking on his feet, the ones he'd hoped to play football with if he made the grade, 'It's hard to say, but I might become Prime Minister.'

Toughnut pondered a while. He'd never in his long tough nut of a career managing umpteen clubs come across such a reply. Most of those he sent packing got jobs packing packets or delivering deliveries not speeches. He raised his eyebrows, looked Pikelet in the eyes and pronounced the now infamous words, 'I'll tell you what Peter. If I were you I'd become Prime Minister and let Tinpot Town do the football.' He thought once more then continued, 'Yes definitely, go into politics … go and run the country. I've watched you in training and apart from your dire performance I've also noticed that you gab on a bit … if I were you I'd become Prime Minister … Chatterboxes have a better chance in politics than at this club where we like stay focused on making sure the ball ends up in the net … How well can you tell lies?'

So it was that Peter Pikelet packed his backpack, the words of Teddy Toughnut ringing in his ears as he made for the exit. 'Don't forget to collect that picture of Betty Skyrocket you pinned up in the locker room. I don't want others getting grand ideas.'

'There *are* Cup Final winners,' Pikelet thought to himself as he picked up his belongings, 'there *are* those who score the winning goal in the final … someone's got to do it.' He then set off to find a profession worthy of his lofty ambitions. 'They'll see. I'll show 'em … They'll live to regret it' swore Pikelet as he set off to have the studs on his boots recycled by the club climate change activist so that they could be used by the next trainee in line.

Cup finals are often given labels that add to their mystique. Such as the 'Bubble Gum Final' which was abandoned after a mass of sticky stuff stuck to the boot of the referee, the 'Escaped Lion Final' in which three spectators were gobbled up before the beast was made to cough them back out alive, the 'Dead Stickleback Final' when a freak storm swept millions of tiny fish onto the pitch to make things slippery, and the 'Swarm of Bees Final' when the players had a sugar rush and began calling each other 'Honey'. Always exciting and often the greatest game in the football calendar that is played at the National Stadium.[1]

It is said that when a man or women does score the winning goal in such a game this can be life changing. Which way depends on whether it is for their own team or a home goal. That winners never have to pay for drinks or an Xmas turkey again. But these sayings were coined

---

1. The dates of these games can be found online by searching The Year Dot.

many years ago and accolades don't pay the rent. Even utility players have utility bills but you could say that folks have cottoned on and when Cup Final heroes enter places where they were once worshipped the punters run for the exits faster than if someone had shouted 'Fire!' Who can forget Wayne Shirt Puller who took the 'free ride' assurance literally and got himself arrested for bilking a taxi driver after asking to be taken on a 300 mile round trip to collect a takeaway from his favourite pizza palace? Another entry in the growing List of Football Casualties Who Had It All and Blew It Away compiled by Professor Naomi Fitz-Nicely of Long Forgotten University.

Many football fans say the greatest Cup Final of all was that in which Royal Warrant Wanderers beat Knockdown Casuals 13-7. Casuals who were 7-0 up at half time got too laid back eating pies during the second half, much of which they spent using the nets as hammocks and snoring loudly. To make matters worse they were given a roasting and for years afterwards players bore griddle marks on their backsides.

Others claim that the greatest game was the clash between Tiptoe Tulips and Bandbox Rovers which ended in a 5-5 draw after extra time plus 103 minutes of stoppage time. Rovers won 111-110 in the penalty shoot-out, a result only confirmed after three recounts and the Director of Sludgetown Symphonia testing the referee's whistle. There is still controversy as to whether Rovers' final penalty-taker smeared the ball with Dragon Grease. No-one will ever know the truth as it was whisked away by a passing albatross. It was also the game in which the VAR system overheated and the goalposts were stolen by souvenir hunters. Some observers described the punch up that took place in the laundry room afterwards as The Rumble by the Tumbledryer.

It's the memorable contributions of individuals that stick in spectators' minds (and sometimes in their throats). They include Dickie Trickie who balanced the ball on his head the length of the pitch before nudging it past the opposing goalkeeper with his left ear. Others recall the wizardry of Sloth Athletic WFC's Freda Silk (aka The Footballing Ballerina) whose pitch length dribbles delighted supporters as she pirouetted the long way round the 18 yard box. Backwards and forwards, up and down, doing a quick jig around each corner flag then at the critical moment, after playing keepy-uppy on the centre spot, letting rip with a shot that traversed the pitch like a bouncing bomb before breaking the back of her own side's net. There are many fans who say 'I was there' but most couldn't have been because the incident happened before the gates were freed up after being glued together by Stop the Football Rot protesters.

Still less perhaps have fans been able to forget the 'Red Card Final' when pitched battles broke out between organizers and match officials so that the players had to escape by helicopter. Others remember Billy Brogan, centre half extraordinaire who played on after breaking a leg and both arms. Brogan's last-minute aerobics, culminating in a double somersault and stretching his one serviceable limb to score, gave his side victory. He'd just done the same nine times in two minutes only to hit the crossbar each time to cries of 'Send for an ambulance!' 'You only live once,' Brogan wrote in his memoirs, *Breaking Bones Without Frontiers,* 'I must have lost the plot after their energetic full back Mohammed Tailspin turned around so quickly he disappeared in a cloud of dust...I knew I'd injured myself quite badly but the real problem was that I had hay fever.'

Ron and Reg Bonehead pulled off the only appearance by identical twins before Jack and Jill Underhill did something similar in a brother-sister combination in the first 'Mixed Doubles Final'. Identical twins can be a problem for referees especially when tracking yellow or red cards. Brother and sister combinations are said to present less of a problem.

Other famous games include the 'Electric Screwdriver Final' in which the Robot triplets, Ice, Twice and Nice, played alongside a centre forward they'd made out of bits of wire and a discarded bedspring. Known due to the success of the accompanying cyber game *Flat Pack Back Three,* the Robots were as impenetrable as Boltdown Mechanics' defence the following year when they held Park the Bus United to a 0-0 draw in the 'Final of Two Dead Ends'. The year Mike Spanner was sent off for nutting Ben Toolbox. Mike was found not to have been registered in time which threw a further spanner in the works.

'Some are born to win,' commented former goalkeeper and sports reporter Peter Dismal.[2] 'I recall it happening in other sports too ... being born ... Born to run, born to be a champion hurdler, born to throw a boomerang ... Like high flying Sandra Solid who whilst being taught to poke a stick at a wasp broke the world record for the pole vault. Or Sol Whippet who ran the 100 metres so fast he went straight through a wall at nursery school. Not unlike César Rapid Brain Swot who beat the grandmaster explaining the moves of chess to him.' It is debatable however whether chess is a sport so that may not count. 'Be things as they may be, there'll always be those born to do something or other,' said Peter Dismal who was in the process of telling listeners that he was born to commentate.

Not everyone can win. Cup Finals are also about losing. It's hard to comprehend the devastation of getting so close to the prize and having it spirited away. Readers may readily understand the lives of winners who live on that glory and leave the game on a high. Less so the trials and tribulations of losers who end up stacking supermarket shelves. But not to end on too downbeat a note, spare a thought for Jamie Tomorrow who won and lost in consecutive years five years running. He once said, 'I don't know if I'm coming or going but I do know where I've been.' He eventually emigrated to the Underside of the Earth where he won the Barbeque Cup, the Jumpalot League and Barrier Cream Trophy.

For many supporters Cup Finals are about the experience, 'the buzz'. The day out, the trip, the dried-out sandwiches, the flask of cold coffee, the extortionate prices at the bar. For those lucky enough to be in the hospitality suites, the champagne, the prawn baguettes and the coronation chicken crisps.

'One thing I've never been able to understand,' commented Peter Dismal. 'Why do those in the posh seats come back late after half time?'

---

2. See Tall Tales Nos. 4 and 6 for Dismal's utterly tedious background.

'Why do Prime Ministers get a seat with a thick cushion,' interrupted Peter Pikelet, Prime Minister, from behind his entourage of security guards.

'Hi Teddy, I made it,' he shouted across to Teddy Toughnut sitting in the You Must Be Vaguely Important section. 'I see Tinpot Town were knocked out in Round One by Minnows United formed just two years ago for a giggle!'

'Pass me that chip I spy on your shoulder,' replied Teddy, 'You were about as good at football as an ice lolly in a microwave … and we all know that any fool in a suit can be PM these days!'

The Eleven Golden Rules of Football

1. Learn to recognise the ball.
2. Avoid pork pies.
3. Don't bank on £5 million a year.
4. Be nice to football psychopaths.
5. Clean the manager's boots.
6. Don't play more than three games a day.
7. Wear a beanie hat in bed.
8. Start out in goal if you really have to.
9. Build a trophy cabinet on the off-chance.
10. Never leave early. Even 0-5 is not irretrievable.
11. Obey rules 1–10 at your own peril.

Play resumes ...

Extra time

I played a time or two when instead of deciding a game within 90 or 120 minutes or with a shoot-out we continued until someone scored a Golden Goal. In contrast to the time we played just 15 minutes before being chased away by an irate groundsman who didn't like the ruts we were making in what he seems to have thought was his well-tended lawn. We shouldn't have been there to begin with but in the days before we had our own ground we sometimes played wherever we saw the opportunity and hoped for the best.

We Lost ... But We Did Play Football

One species I haven't mentioned beginning with P is the lesser-spotted philosopher. Occasionally glimpsed on street corners in the Potted North but by the thousand at places like Oakwell on match days, this strange animal would come out with lots of things to do with the meaning of life. Maybe it's the same in London's East End (where they have a penchant for rhyming slang), on Tyneside, Merseyside, or in Glasgow. Homespun and with deep meaning like 'There's now't so queer as folk' or 'Everything happens for a reason' not clever stuff comparing dandelion and burdock to a four dimensional worm through time.[1] Things like 'We may lose but we do play football', a phrase to let the hopeless know they still have hope.

---

1. Emmanuel Kant. But for the dandelion and burdock and no relation to N'Golo Kanté the Chelsea and Al-Ittihad player whose name has a posh é.

Earlier in the book, I mentioned the 'Ponty End' at Oakwell. It's become the Norman Rimmington Stand. He was the archetype football stalwart and there's something of 'Rimmo' in my stories. A supporter, an apprentice, back room boy, trainee, first team goalkeeper, assistant manager, groundsman, physio, kit man, laundry supervisor and general factotum he outlived many who passed through the club and died aged 93 still helping out. There are also shades of someone less known for his football than his athleticism who (as Barry Hines did) played for Barnsley Reserves. Arthur Rowe won Gold Medals putting the shot at the British Empire and Commonwealth Games and the European Athletics Championship.[2] He beat mesmerised kilt-wearing locals at Scotland's Highland Games (having only seen pictures in books) and represented Great Britain at the Rome Olympics (having never wandered beyond the back garden except when throwing things huge distances).[3] He's credited with being one of two blokes who lifted a car out of a swamp with their bare hands after a forklift truck was defeated. His subconscious influences on my writing stem from a legend that the first time he picked up the shot he broke the world record.[4]

You will I hope recognise things I've written about. People and places you know or have seen. I'd be surprised if you haven't wanted to get the autographs of footballers like Betty Skyrocket and Stanley Accrington. You may recall meeting a fourth string goalie who was never called on to play, put your foot in it by asking a question before first checking out the answer (as I did with poor Jimmy Baxter), or listening to commentators who've lost the plot.

2. Still the only person to do this in the same year.
3. The Commonwealth and Europe in 1958 and the Olympics in 1960.
4. The truth is Rowe might never have been an Olympian had he not aged 17 been waiting to bat at cricket. New to him, he saw men putting the shot and asked if he could try it. He beat them all by over two metres.

Squeaky bum time

What else sticks in my mind that might have seeped into my subconscious and shaped the stories in this book? I once entered the packed lift of a London hotel to find myself chest-to-chest with the towering presence of England and Liverpool goalkeeper Ray Clemence, so I know what it's like to be in a tight squeeze or a high press. I've jumped from side to side on the pavement to let Alan Shearer pass more than once but he wouldn't know me other than as a local when he stayed nearby. A Premier League footballer tried to buy the house next door to us. He wanted to install a security system that would have left President Vladimir Putin of Russia wondering about the cost and I've used the same fish and chip shop that Harry Redknapp does in Sandbanks, Dorset, the Amalfi Coast of Britain.

Years ago, I stood in a thick overcoat and watched Everton win 3-0 at Oakwell after the pitch, which had been covered in six inches of snow, was rolled flat and the teams played on what turned into packed ice. At Bradford City's ground, under primitive floodlights, the rain was so torrential and the puddles so deep that it was impossible to distinguish the players from drowning rats. I think local artist David Hockney must have been in the crowd because he painted a picture called 'The Splash' which changed hands at Sotheby's for £23.1 million. That's about a year's wages for an average Premier League player.

I was once taken by Uncle Jeremiah (the one who sold dud footballs and rented out bodyguards) to Hillsborough to watch an 'exhibition game' between Sheffield Wednesday and Moscow Torpedo, only to be ungrateful and say, 'I'd have preferred it to have been Moscow Dynamo' who were more famous at the time. I sat two seats away from Michael Parkinson on a cold day at Reading's Elm Park, now houses and flats, when he wore a sheepskin coat so thick it must have used up the flock, and I saw Barnsley lose 7-0 there on a 'bad day for the Tykes' when, by the end, I was the only one in the away end. Another day a Japanese fellow bounced the ball on his head without a break throughout half time. It was more interesting than the 0-0 draw.

I'll allow myself one farewell tale. One Boxing Day in the Potted North we couldn't find a match to go to. Barnsley were playing Hartlepool United (a 200 mile round trip) and tickets at Hillsborough and Elland Road had sold out to those with more nous then to leave it to the last minute. Except for one game. Emley AFC were playing at Wakefield Trinity rugby league club's former home Belle Vue. In the days before soccer went wall-to-wall on TV, due to official concerns supporters wouldn't attend live matches, Rugby League was king. A main attraction for couch lizards. Still recovering from being sent off at rugby even I'd seen it from the corner of one eye.

We drove to the checkpoint on the border between South and West Yorkshire, showed our passports, turned out our pockets, bribed the guards with mince pies and threw the dog a turkey bone before driving on to Belle Vue. It looked smaller than it had seemed on TV but still had its old grandstand.[5] The crowd was just a couple of hundred and the players seemed tiny from the high bank where we stood watching. I can't recall the score but I remember kicking every ball.

I don't normally collect memorabilia but I came away with an Emley AFC scarf in powder blue and maroon (the same as at Burnley, Aston Villa and West Ham United). I bought it from the 'club shop' a trestle table by one of the goals. It could've been the Bernabeu, San Siro or The Emirates. It didn't matter. It was football. That's what being a fan is all about (and what 'we' ex-players can't resist revisiting). What's more, we were a stone's throw from where Dennis Law kept me out of the Huddersfield Town side. I kept quiet about that though as I chatted with the friendly lady on the stall.

> **FINAL WHISTLE!** Time for a nice hot bath… or should that be an ice cold shower?

---

5.   In their present incarnation Emley AFC play at the Welfare Ground, a stadium nearby. See https://www.emleyafc.co.uk/

Acknowledgements

I'm tempted, as Spike Milligan did when handed a Lifetime Achievement Award, to say 'I did it all myself'. It wouldn't be true. I had to correct the manuscript after being informed that names I'd used for characters, clubs or events existed in real life. Some things needed updating and there turned out to be so many kinds of football that some of my Strange Games had to be airbrushed. Nowadays clubs often have colourful labels so it's harder to come up with fictional ones. Like those in the First Qualifying Round of this year's FA Cup: Sporting Bengal United, Roman Glass St George, Aylesbury Vale Dynamo, New Salamis and Crook Town. The last of these should play the Grimsby Police XI.

Michael Parkinson's *Football Daft* contains tales of Skinner Normanton 'the only man born with a pointed head' who trained by running up Mount Everest backwards carrying two buckets of cement. Others like Chick Farr, the Bradford Park Avenue goalie, who saved effort pulling down the crossbar rather than jumping for the ball. I'm indebted to the late Sir Michael as I am to Ian McMillan who's written in a similar tongue in cheek way including his *Yorkshire Fairy Tales*. I particularly enjoyed his other story about the conductor on the Trans Pennine Express who told passengers he was really a fully-qualified landscape gardener (I've met a few of those). As I said early on we're all three from a place teeming with poets, playwrights and performers.

I'm also grateful for the keen humour of two departed friends. Singer, actor and broadcaster Tony Capstick whose monologue on his hit record *Sheffield Grinder/Capstick Comes Home* is sheer poetic exaggeration: 'When I were a lad you could get a tram down into t'town, buy three new suits an' an overcoat, four pair o' good boots … get blind drunk, 'ave some steak an' chips, bunch o' bananas an' three stone o' monkey nuts an' still 'ave change out of a farthing'. When Sheffield Wednesday beat Manchester United 1-0 to unexpectedly win the League Cup, Tony led the community singing.[1]

Nicholas J Stevens was a lawyer friend who with myself and others founded The Apostrophe Club to spot rogue examples of these creatures in news outlets such as the *Banbury Cake, Carlisle Mosquito* and *Royston Crow*.[2] Writer, sometime poet and club scribe he recorded our correspondence with such phantom contacts as The Right Honourable Colonel Double-Yoke of the Brigade of Semi-Colons. I see there's even a fake report about a chap who believed his marriage licence covered the TV, driving a bus, fishing and keeping an iguana.

My thanks also go to Peter Cook (and E L Wisty); The Four Yorkshiremen of Beyond the Fringe; Harry Enfield's bluff Yorkshire businessman: 'Sophistication, sophistication. Don't talk to me about sophistication … A've bin to Leeds'; Monty Python; celluloid mockumentaries such as *A Mighty Wind, This is Spinal Tap* and *Best In Show*; and the anonymous individuals behind my characters.

Finally, a big thank you to John Cooper, who turned parts of the text into such telling images, and Alex Gibson who pieced the whole book together at Waterside Press.

Bryan Gibson
September 2023

---

1. Wembley Stadium 1991 when Tony stood on a podium in a white suit, guitar in hand, as he led the crowd singing soccer anthems. Or did I dream this?
2. All real. *The Mosquito* is a newspaper in the USA, the others in England.

Index (including key fictional items)

Good Moaning France!

Officer Crabtree's Fronch Phrose Berk

by Arthur Bostrom, Foreword by Rick Wakeman

Based on a favourite character from BBC TV sitcom *'Allo 'Allo!*
In this delightful book, Officer Crabtree's masterly grasp of Fronch falls
under the spotlight as never before. From '*Ploose may I hov a kippy of the
dooly nosepooper?*' to '*frigs logs*', '*scrimbled oggs*' and '*fosh and chops*' the
book is a tribute to mangled words and phrases. Arthur Bostrom, who
played Officer Crabtree on stage and screen, mixes vowels and pronuncia-
tion trying to educate those less gifted in the French *longwodge*.

'Listen very carefully, you will read this more than once. I *loaved* it'
Les Dennis

Paperback & ebook | ISBN 978-1-909976-59-7

www.WatersidePress.co.uk